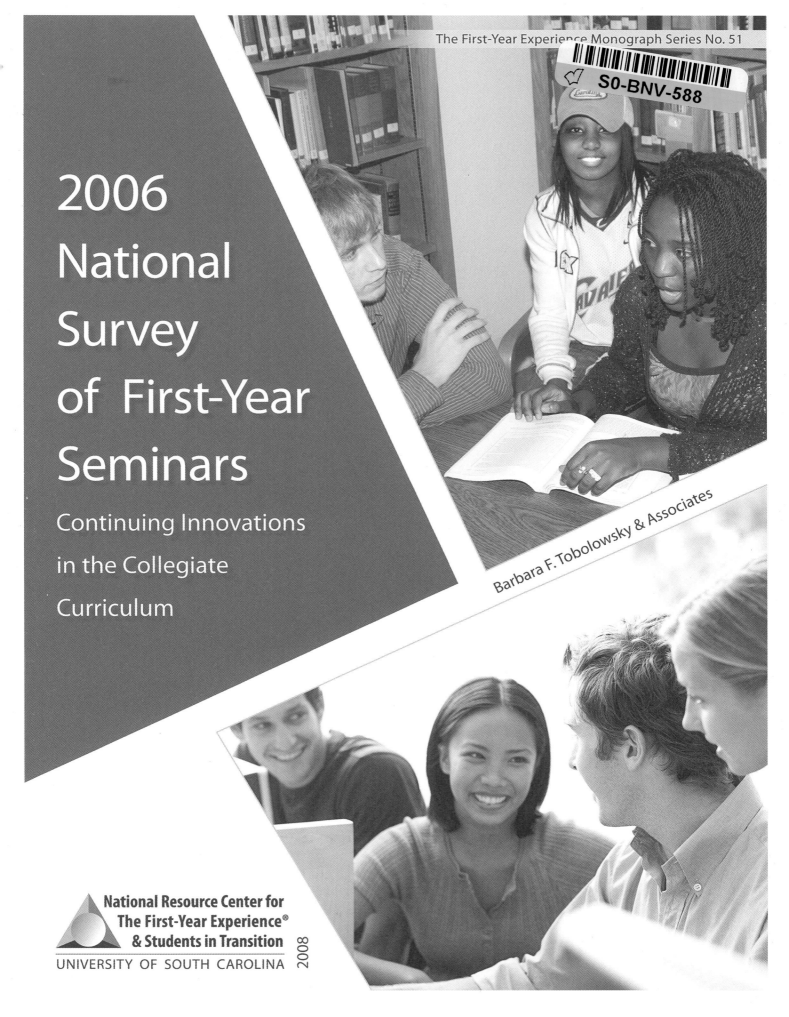

S0-BNV-588

2006 National Survey of First-Year Seminars

Continuing Innovations in the Collegiate Curriculum

Barbara F. Tobolowsky & Associates

National Resource Center for The First-Year Experience® & Students in Transition

UNIVERSITY OF SOUTH CAROLINA

2008

Cite as:

Tobolowsky, B. F., & Associates. (2008). *2006 National Survey of First-Year Seminars: Continuing innovations in the collegiate curriculum* (Monograph No. 51). Columbia, SC: University of South Carolina, National Resource Center for The First-Year Experience and Students in Transition.

Sample chapter citation:

Schryer, A., Griffin A., & Tobolowsky, B. F. (2008). Methodology and institutional characteristics. In B. F. Tobolowsky & Associates, *2006 National Survey of First-Year Seminars: Continuing innovations in the collegiate curriculum* (Monograph No. 51, pp. 5-9). Columbia, SC: University of South Carolina, National Resource Center for The First-Year Experience and Students in Transition.

ISBN 978-1-889-27164-4

Special thanks to Tracy L. Skipper, Editorial Projects Coordinator, and Dottie Weigel, Graduate Assistant, for copyediting and proofing; and to Angie Mellor, Graphic Artist for design and layout.

Additional copies of this monograph may be obtained from the National Resource Center for The First-Year Experience and Students in Transition, University of South Carolina, 1728 College Street, Columbia, SC 29208. Telephone (803) 777-6229. Fax (803) 777-4699.

Library of Congress Cataloging-in-Publication Data

Tobolowsky, Barbara F.
   2006 national survey of first-year seminars : continuing innovations in the collegiate curriculum / Barbara F. Tobolowsky & associates.
      p. cm. -- (The first-year experience monograph series ; no. 51)
   Includes bibliographical references.
   ISBN 978-1-889271-64-4
 1. College student development programs--United States--Evaluation. 2. College freshmen--United States. 3. Seminars--United States--Evaluation. 4. National Survey of First-Year Seminar Programming. 5. Educational surveys--United States. I. Title.

 LB2343.4.T55 2008
 378.1'98--dc22
                              2008037410

Contents

List of Tables v

Introduction
Barbara F. Tobolowsky xi

Chapter 1
An Historical Perspective on First-Year Seminars
Dana Fish Saunders and Jonathan Romm 1

Chapter 2
Methodology and Institutional Characteristics
Asheley Schryer, Angela Griffin, and Barbara F. Tobolowsky 5

Chapter 3
The First-Year Seminar Characteristics
Angela Griffin, Jonathan Romm, and Barbara F. Tobolowsky 11

Chapter 4
Seminar Instruction and Training
Barbara F. Tobolowsky and Angela Griffin 63

Chapter 5
Course Objectives and Assessment
Angela Griffin and Barbara F. Tobolowsky 83

Chapter 6
Summary of Selected Findings
Barbara F. Tobolowsky 97

About the Contributors 103

Appendix A
2006 National Survey of First-Year Seminars 105

Appendix B
List of Participating Institutions 115

List of Tables

Table 2.1   *Characteristics of Responding Institutions With Seminars* 7

Table 2.2   *Undergraduate Headcount at Two-Year Institutions* 7

Table 2.3   *Undergraduate Headcount at Four-Year Institutions* 8

Table 2.4   *Representation of 2006 Survey Respondents Compared to National Average*
by Institutional Type and Size 8

Table 3.1   *Seminar Longevity Across All Institutions* 11

Table 3.2   *Seminar Longevity by Institutional Affiliation* 12

Table 3.3   *Seminar Longevity by Institutional Type* 12

Table 3.4   *Seminar Longevity by Institutional Selectivity* 12

Table 3.5   *Seminar Longevity by Institutional Size* 12

Table 3.6   *Seminar Longevity by Seminar Type* 13

Table 3.7   *Respondents Offering Each Type of Seminar Across All Institutions* 14

Table 3.8   *Percentage of Respondents Offering Each Type of Seminar by Institutional Affiliation* 14

Table 3.9   *Percentage of Respondents Offering Each Type of Seminar by Institutional Type* 15

Table 3.10   *Percentage of Respondents Offering Each Type of Seminar by Institutional Selectivity* 15

Table 3.11   *Percentage of Respondents Offering Each Type of Seminar by Institutional Size.* 16

Table 3.12   *Respondents' Primary Seminar Type Across All Institutions* 16

Table 3.13   *Percentage of Respondents Reporting Primary Seminar Type by Institutional Affiliation.* . . . 17

Table 3.14   *Percentage of Respondents Reporting Primary Seminar Type by Institutional Type* 17

Table 3.15   *Percentage of Respondents Reporting Primary Seminar Type by Institutional Selectivity* . . . 17

Table 3.16   *Percentage of Respondents Reporting Primary Seminar Type by Institutional Size.* 18

Table 3.17   *Online-Only Seminar Sections Across All Institutions* 19

Table 3.18   *Online-Only Seminar Sections by Institutional Affiliation* 19

Table 3.19   *Online-Only Seminar Sections by Institutional Type* 19

Table 3.20   *Online-Only Seminar Sections by Institutional Selectivity* 19

Table 3.21   *Online-Only Seminar Sections by Institutional Size* 19

Table 3.22   *Online-Only Seminar Sections by Seminar Type* 20

Table 3.23   *Seminar Includes Online Components Across All Institutions* 20

Table 3.24   *Seminar Includes Online Components by Institutional Affiliation* 20

Table 3.25   *Seminar Includes Online Components by Institutional Type* 20

Table 3.26   *Seminar Includes Online Components by Institutional Selectivity* 20

Table 3.27   *Seminar Includes Online Components by Institutional Size* 21

Table 3.28   *Seminar Includes Online Components by Seminar Type* 21

Table 3.29   *Seminar Is Part of Learning Community Across All Institutions* 22

Table 3.30   *Seminar Is Part of Learning Community by Institutional Affiliation* 22

Table 3.31   *Seminar Is Part of Learning Community by Institutional Type* 22
Table 3.32   *Seminar Is Part of Learning Community by Institutional Selectivity* 22
Table 3.33   *Seminar Is Part of Learning Community by Institutional Size* 22
Table 3.34   *Seminar Is Part of Learning Community by Seminar Type* 23
Table 3.35   *Seminar Includes Service-Learning Component Across All Institutions* 23
Table 3.36   *Seminar Includes Service-Learning Component by Institutional Affiliation* 24
Table 3.37   *Seminar Includes Service-Learning Component by Institutional Type* 24
Table 3.38   *Seminar Includes Service-Learning Component by Institutional Selectivity* 24
Table 3.39   *Seminar Includes Service-Learning Component by Institutional Size* 24
Table 3.40   *Seminar Includes Service-Learning Component by Seminar Type* 24
Table 3.41   *Percentage of Respondents Reporting Approximate Class Size Across All Institutions* 25
Table 3.42   *Percentage of Respondents Reporting Approximate Class Size by Institutional Affiliation* . . . 25
Table 3.43   *Percentage of Respondents Reporting Approximate Class Size by Institutional Type* 26
Table 3.44   *Percentage of Respondents Reporting Approximate Class Size by Institutional Selectivity* . . . 26
Table 3.45   *Percentage of Respondents Reporting Approximate Class Size by Institutional Size* 26
Table 3.46   *Percentage of Respondents Reporting Approximate Class Size by Seminar Type* 27
Table 3.47   *Seminar Length Across All Institutions* 27
Table 3.48   *Seminar Length by Institutional Affiliation* 27
Table 3.49   *Seminar Length by Institutional Type* 28
Table 3.50   *Seminar Length by Institutional Selectivity* 28
Table 3.51   *Seminar Length by Institutional Size.* 28
Table 3.52   *Seminar Length by Seminar Type* 29
Table 3.53   *Percentage of First-Year Students Required to Take Seminar Across All Institutions* 29
Table 3.54   *Percentage of First-Year Students Required to Take Seminar by Institutional Affiliation.* . . . 30
Table 3.55   *Percentage of First-Year Students Required to Take Seminar by Institutional Type* 30
Table 3.56   *Percentage of First-Year Students Required to Take Seminar by Institutional Selectivity.* . . . 31
Table 3.57   *Percentage of First-Year Students Required to Take Seminar by Institutional Size.* 31
Table 3.58   *Percentage of First-Year Students Required to Take Seminar Size by Seminar Type* 32
Table 3.59   *Type of Students Required to Take Seminar Across All Institutions* 32
Table 3.60   *Type of Students Required to Take Seminar by Institutional Affiliation* 33
Table 3.61   *Type of Students Required to Take Seminar by Institutional Type* 33
Table 3.62   *Type of Students Required to Take Seminar by Institutional Selectivity* 34
Table 3.63   *Type of Students Required to Take Seminar by Institutional Size.* 34
Table 3.64   *Type of Students Required to Take Seminar by Seminar Type* 35
Table 3.65   *Percentage of Special Sections Offered Across All Institutions* 36
Table 3.66   *Percentage of Special Sections Offered by Institutional Affiliation* 36
Table 3.67   *Percentage of Special Sections Offered by Institutional Type* 37
Table 3.68   *Percentage of Special Sections Offered by Institutional Selectivity* 38
Table 3.69   *Percentage of Special Sections Offered by Institutional Size* 39
Table 3.70   *Percentage of Seminars That Carry Credit Toward Graduation Across All Institutions* 40
Table 3.71   *Percentage of Seminars That Carry Credit Toward Graduation by Institutional Affiliation* . . 40
Table 3.72   *Percentage of Seminars That Carry Credit Toward Graduation by Institutional Type* 40
Table 3.73   *Percentage of Seminars That Carry Credit Toward Graduation by Institutional Selectivity* . . 40

Table 3.74   *Percentage of Seminars That Carry Credit Toward Graduation by Institutional Size* 40
Table 3.75   *Percentage of Seminars That Carry Credit Toward Graduation by Seminar Type* 41
Table 3.76   *Credit Hours Offered Across All Institutions* 41
Table 3.77   *Credit Hours Offered by Institutional Affiliation* 41
Table 3.78   *Credit Hours Offered by Institutional Type* 42
Table 3.79   *Credit Hours Offered by Institutional Selectivity* 42
Table 3.80   *Credit Hours Offered by Institutional Size* 42
Table 3.81   *Credit Hours Offered by Seminar Type* 43
Table 3.82   *Application of Credit Across All Institutions* 43
Table 3.83   *Application of Credit by Institutional Affiliation* 43
Table 3.84   *Application of Credit by Institutional Type* 44
Table 3.85   *Application of Credit by Institutional Selectivity* 44
Table 3.86   *Application of Credit by Institutional Size* 44
Table 3.87   *Application of Credit by Seminar Type* 45
Table 3.88   *Method of Grading Across All Institutions* 45
Table 3.89   *Method of Grading by Institutional Affiliation* 45
Table 3.90   *Method of Grading by Institutional Type* 46
Table 3.91   *Method of Grading by Institutional Selectivity* 46
Table 3.92   *Method of Grading by Institutional Size* 46
Table 3.93   *Method of Grading by Seminar Type* 46
Table 3.94   *Contact Hours per Week Across All Institutions* 47
Table 3.95   *Contact Hours per Week by Institutional Affiliation* 47
Table 3.96   *Contact Hours per Week by Institutional Type* 48
Table 3.97   *Contact Hours per Week by Institutional Selectivity* 48
Table 3.98   *Contact Hours per Week by Institutional Size* 48
Table 3.99   *Contact Hours per Week by Seminar Type* 49
Table 3.100   *Most Important Course Topics Across All Institutions* 50
Table 3.101   *Most Important Course Topics by Institutional Affiliation* 50
Table 3.102   *Most Important Course Topics by Institutional Type* 51
Table 3.103   *Most Important Course Topics by Institutional Selectivity* 51
Table 3.104   *Most Important Course Topics by Institutional Size* 52
Table 3.105   *Most Important Course Topics by Seminar Type* 53
Table 3.106   *Administrative Home of First-Year Seminar Across All Institutions* 54
Table 3.107   *Administrative Home of First-Year Seminar by Institutional Affiliation* 54
Table 3.108   *Administrative Home of First-Year Seminar by Institutional Type* 54
Table 3.109   *Administrative Home of First-Year Seminar by Institutional Selectivity* 55
Table 3.110   *Administrative Home of First-Year Seminar by Institutional Size* 55
Table 3.111   *Administrative Home of First-Year Seminar by Seminar Type* 55
Table 3.112   *Seminar Has Dean/Director/Coordinator Across All Institutions* 56
Table 3.113   *Seminar Has Dean/Director/Coordinator by Institutional Affiliation* 56
Table 3.114   *Seminar Has Dean/Director/Coordinator by Institutional Type* 56
Table 3.115   *Seminar Has Dean/Director/Coordinator by Institutional Selectivity* 56
Table 3.116   *Seminar Has Dean/Director/Coordinator by Institutional Size* 57

Table 3.117   *Seminar Has Dean/Director/Coordinator by Seminar Type* 57

Table 3.118   *Status of Dean/Director/Coordinator Across All Institutions* 57

Table 3.119   *Status of Dean/Director/Coordinator by Institutional Affiliation* 57

Table 3.120   *Status of Dean/Director/Coordinator by Institutional Type* 57

Table 3.121   *Status of Dean/Director/Coordinator by Institutional Selectivity* 58

Table 3.122   *Status of Dean/Director/Coordinator by Institutional Size* 58

Table 3.123   *Status of Dean/Director/Coordinator by Seminar Type* 58

Table 3.124   *Other Role of Dean/Director/Coordinator Across All Institutions* 58

Table 3.125   *Other Role of Dean/Director/Coordinator by Institutional Affiliation* 59

Table 3.126   *Other Role of Dean/Director/Coordinator by Institutional Type* 59

Table 3.127   *Other Role of Dean/Director/Coordinator by Institutional Selectivity* 59

Table 3.128   *Other Role of Dean/Director/Coordinator by Institutional Size* 60

Table 3.129   *Other Role of Dean/Director/Coordinator by Seminar Type* 60

Table 4.1   *Teaching Responsibility Across All Institutions* 63

Table 4.2   *Teaching Responsibility by Institutional Affiliation* 64

Table 4.3   *Teaching Responsibility by Institutional Type* 64

Table 4.4   *Teaching Responsibility by Institutional Selectivity* 64

Table 4.5   *Teaching Responsibility by Institutional Size* 65

Table 4.6   *Teaching Responsibility by Seminar Type* 65

Table 4.7   *Percentage of Institutions Reporting Team-Taught Sections Across All Institutions* 66

Table 4.8   *Percentage of Institutions Reporting Team-Taught Sections by Institutional Affiliation* 66

Table 4.9   *Percentage of Institutions Reporting Team-Taught Sections by Institutional Type* 66

Table 4.10   *Percentage of Institutions Reporting Team-Taught Sections by Institutional Selectivity* 67

Table 4.11   *Percentage of Institutions Reporting Team-Taught Sections by Institutional Size* 67

Table 4.12   *Percentage of Institutions Reporting Team-Taught Sections by Seminar Type* 67

Table 4.13   *Percentage of Students Enrolled in Team-Taught Sections Across All Institutions* 67

Table 4.14   *Percentage of Students Enrolled in Team-Taught Sections by Institutional Affiliation* 68

Table 4.15   *Percentage of Students Enrolled in Team-Taught Sections by Institutional Type* 68

Table 4.16   *Percentage of Students Enrolled in Team-Taught Sections by Institutional Selectivity* 68

Table 4.17   *Percentage of Students Enrolled in Team-Taught Sections by Institutional Size* 69

Table 4.18   *Percentage of Students Enrolled in Team-Taught Sections by Seminar Type* 69

Table 4.19   *Institutions With Sections Taught by Academic Advisor Across All Institutions* 69

Table 4.20   *Institutions With Sections Taught by Academic Advisor by Institutional Affiliation* 70

Table 4.21   *Institutions With Sections Taught by Academic Advisor by Institutional Type* 70

Table 4.22   *Institutions With Sections Taught by Academic Advisor by Institutional Selectivity* 70

Table 4.23   *Institutions With Sections Taught by Academic Advisor by Institutional Size* 70

Table 4.24   *Institutions With Sections Taught by Academic Advisor by Seminar Type* 71

Table 4.25   *Faculty Workload Configuration Across All Institutions* 72

Table 4.26   *Faculty Workload Configuration by Institutional Affiliation* 72

Table 4.27   *Faculty Workload Configuration by Institutional Type* 72

Table 4.28   *Faculty Workload Configuration by Institutional Selectivity* 72

Table 4.29   *Faculty Workload Configuration by Institutional Size* 73

Table 4.30   *Faculty Workload Configuration by Seminar Type* 73

Table 4.31   *Administrative Staff Workload Configuration Across All Institutions* 73
Table 4.32   *Administrative Staff Workload Configuration by Institutional Affiliation* 73
Table 4.33   *Administrative Staff Workload Configuration by Institutional Type* 74
Table 4.34   *Administrative Staff Workload Configuration by Institutional Selectivity* 74
Table 4.35   *Administrative Staff Workload Configuration by Institutional Size* 74
Table 4.36   *Administrative Staff Workload Configuration by Seminar Type* 74
Table 4.37   *Instructor Compensation Across All Institutions* 75
Table 4.38   *Instructor Compensation by Institutional Affiliation* 75
Table 4.39   *Instructor Compensation by Institutional Type* 75
Table 4.40   *Instructor Compensation by Institutional Selectivity* 75
Table 4.41   *Instructor Compensation by Institutional Size* 76
Table 4.42   *Instructor Compensation by Seminar Type* 76
Table 4.43   *Faculty Workload Configuration by Instructor Compensation* 76
Table 4.44   *Administrative Staff Workload Configuration by Instructor Compensation* 77
Table 4.45   *Instructor Training Offered Across All Institutions.* 77
Table 4.46   *Instructor Training Offered by Institutional Affiliation* 77
Table 4.47   *Instructor Training Offered by Institutional Type* 78
Table 4.48   *Instructor Training Offered by Institutional Selectivity* 78
Table 4.49   *Instructor Training Offered by Institutional Size* 78
Table 4.50   *Instructor Training Offered by Seminar Type* 78
Table 4.51   *Instructor Training Required Across All Institutions* 78
Table 4.52   *Instructor Training Required by Institutional Affiliation* 79
Table 4.53   *Instructor Training Required by Institutional Type* 79
Table 4.54   *Instructor Training Required by Institutional Selectivity* 79
Table 4.55   *Instructor Training Required by Institutional Size* 79
Table 4.56   *Instructor Training Required by Seminar Type* 79
Table 4.57   *Length of Instructor Training Across All Institutions* 80
Table 4.58   *Length of Instructor Training by Institutional Affiliation* 80
Table 4.59   *Length of Instructor Training by Institutional Type* 80
Table 4.60   *Length of Instructor Training by Institutional Selectivity* 81
Table 4.61   *Length of Instructor Training by Institutional Size* 81
Table 4.62   *Length of Instructor Training by Seminar Type* 82
Table 5.1   *Most Important Course Objectives Across All Institutions* 84
Table 5.2   *Most Important Course Objectives by Institutional Affiliation* 84
Table 5.3   *Most Important Course Objectives by Institutional Type* 85
Table 5.4   *Most Important Course Objectives by Institutional Selectivity* 85
Table 5.5   *Most Important Course Objectives by Institutional Size* 86
Table 5.6   *Most Important Course Objectives by Seminar Type* 87
Table 5.7   *Types of Evaluation Methods Across All Institutions* 88
Table 5.8   *Types of Evaluation Methods by Institutional Affiliation* 88
Table 5.9   *Types of Evaluation Methods by Institutional Type* 89
Table 5.10   *Types of Evaluation Methods by Institutional Selectivity.* 89
Table 5.11   *Types of Evaluation Methods by Institutional Size* 90

Table 5.12   *Types of Evaluation Methods by Seminar Type* 90
Table 5.13   *Results Attributed to First-Year Seminar Across All Institutions* 91
Table 5.14   *Results Attributed to First-Year Seminars by Institutional Affiliation* 92
Table 5.15   *Results Attributed to First-Year Seminars by Institutional Type* 92
Table 5.16   *Results Attributed to First-Year Seminars by Institutional Selectivity* 93
Table 5.17   *Results Attributed to First-Year Seminar by Institutional Size* 94
Table 5.18   *Results Attributed to First-Year Seminar by Seminar Type* 95
Table 6.1   *Comparison of Institutions Offering First-year Seminars, 1988-2006* 99
Table 6.2   *Comparison of Survey Results, 1988-2006* 100

Introduction

In 1988, the National Resource Center for The Freshman Year Experience (as it was known then) conducted the first National Survey of Freshman Seminar Programming. Although the University of South Carolina's first-year seminar had existed since 1972, the Center was still a relatively new entity. With its establishment, a significant literature base was born under John Gardner's guidance and the research and publication efforts of Paul and Dorothy Fidler, Stuart Hunter, and Betsy Barefoot.

It is hard to imagine that was 20 years ago. Much has changed since then. The seminar began with an uncertain future but has become institutionalized on many campuses across the nation. The National Resource Center has experienced a name and leadership change as well as the expansion of its mission. However, over these 20 plus years, one thing has not changed: Every three years, the Center conducts a national survey on first-year seminars—and 2006 was no exception.

The 2006 National Survey on First-Year Seminars remained relatively unchanged, since its major overhaul in 2003, but there were new players. This time, Valarie Redman and Asheley Bice Schryer, graduate assistants at the National Resource Center, worked with me to handle the task of conducting the seventh triennial survey. (See Appendix A for the survey instrument.) Although we contracted with Educational Benchmarking Incorporated (EBI) to administer the survey, there was still a lot of work that Valarie, Asheley, and I did here at the Center regarding its release. By 2007, Valarie and Asheley had moved on. Angela Griffin, the Center's new coordinator of research, grants, and assessment, and Dana Fish Saunders and Jonathan Romm, our graduate assistants in 2007-2008, were on board to assist in survey analysis and contribute to this monograph. I want to thank all of them for their assistance.

Many other people contributed to the execution of the survey and this analysis as well. First, let me thank Tonya Stoll and Rachel Farmer of EBI for their assistance in the nuts and bolts of the administration. Thanks to Marla Mamrick, who conducted the statistical analysis of the data. Thanks also to Betsy Barefoot and Jennifer Keup for their review of this monograph. Betsy has been closely involved with the survey instrument from those early days and continues to be a national advocate for first-year students in her role as co-director and senior scholar at the Policy Center on the First Year of College. Jennifer Keup reviewed the 2003 survey monograph when she was working at the Higher Education Research Institute at UCLA and, at the time of this writing, is beginning her tenure as the director of the National Resource Center.

Most specifically, I want to thank all of the responding institutions. This survey is only useful if there are individuals willing to take the time and effort to participate. We are indebted to you for your support. We also thank everyone who works with first-year students, because it is your work that encourages us in our efforts every day. Finally, I want to thank first-year students who inspire us all. We are dedicated to helping you succeed.

As you can see, many people contributed to the 2006 survey, and this monograph is a reflection of their efforts. To that end, let me thank the Center publication staff, Tracy Skipper, Dottie Weigel, and Angie Mellor, who did the copyediting, layout, and design of this monograph. They always work miracles, and they did it once again with this work.

For those of you who have seen previous survey monographs, this one looks different. In response to your comments and questions since the publication of the 2003 survey monograph, we added more tables to the monograph. In this edition, we have consistently included tables reflecting data in aggregate and by institutional affiliation (i.e., type and control), size, selectivity, and seminar type. In the 2003 survey monograph, we separated the qualitative data from the quantitative data, but we decided to report both together this time. As a result of the increased numbers of tables and rich narrative data, the monograph has a new organization, which we hope will make it easier to navigate and provide a complete and compelling picture of first-year seminars. Therefore, in chapter 1, Dana Fish Saunders and Jonathan Romm provide a brief history of the seminar. In chapter 2, Asheley Bice Schryer, Angela Griffin, and I provide information about the survey methodology and the characteristics of the participating institutions. In chapter 3, Angela Griffin, Jonathan Romm, and I provide the complete profile of the course including the course length, credits offered, topics covered, administration, and successful or innovative course elements. Angela Griffin and I focus on seminar instruction and training in chapter 4 and on learning objectives and assessment in chapter 5. In the final chapter, chapter 6, I offer a summary of key findings from the 2006 survey administration and seminar trends from all the survey iterations from 1988 to 2006. The appendices include the survey instrument and the list of participating institutions that allowed us to share their data.

We hope that the information contained in this monograph continues to help you as you garner support for your efforts on behalf of first-year students while developing, expanding, or institutionalizing the first-year seminar on your campuses.

Barbara F. Tobolowsky
Associate Director
National Resource Center for The First-Year Experience and Students in Transition
May, 2008

Chapter 1

An Historical Perspective on First-Year Seminars

Dana Fish Saunders and Jonathan Romm

While first-year college students have always had transitional needs and concerns, higher education did not formally address them until the late 1800s. Though the specifics are unknown, the first reported first-year seminar was in 1882 at Lee College in Kentucky (Barefoot & Fidler, 1996). Boston College is often credited as offering the first extended orientation seminar in 1888, which sought to guide first-year students in their transition to college life, specifically targeting students' academic success (Gahagan, 2002).

The early 20th century ushered in the in loco parentis[1] era, which established institutions' responsibility to guide students' social adjustment as well as individual collegiate success (Mamrick, 2005). As a result, practitioners focused their attention on holistic student development. With this added sense of institutional duty came an obligation to redefine the ultimate mission and goals of first-year seminar courses. By the 1920s and 1930s, the seminar continued to aid students with their academic transitions but placed a new emphasis on students' personal and social challenges. In 1926, more than half of the seminars focused on "adjustment," instead of the traditional "how to study in college" curriculum (Gordon, 1989). More specifically, these courses highlighted the purpose of college, the challenges of the curriculum, student honesty, student government, athletics, morality, and religion. Over the next decade, both the curriculum and the number of first-year seminars continued to grow. By 1930, more than one third of all institutions had incorporated a first-year seminar into the educational curriculum (Gordon).

However, by the late 1930s, things had changed. The faculty had become increasingly frustrated with "life adjustment content" of the curriculum, and fewer could be recruited to teach the course. Consequently, the seminar declined in popularity. By the 1960s, universities had moved completely away from the in loco parentis philosophy, and first-year seminar courses became nearly nonexistent (Drake, 1966). Instead, colleges adopted a "sink or swim" attitude toward first-year students (Gahagan, 2002), which led the students to turn to each other for support as they transitioned to college life (Gordon, 1989).

This attitude continued for more than a decade until the early 1970s, when several factors influenced a reintroduction of first-year seminars into university culture. First, changes in university admissions criteria now allowed access to students who had previously been excluded from college entry. Second, these students often arrived on campus without the necessary "skills of studyhood" (Cohen & Jody, 1978,

p. 2). As a result, remedial courses were added to the university curriculum to address these needs, which inadvertently created a more complex educational system for students to navigate. With this combination of factors, the hands-off attitude of the 1960s was "no longer ethically or economically viable" (Gahagan, 2002, p. 5), and first-year seminars slowly began to reemerge on college and university campuses.

In the late 1960s and early 1970s, student political unrest, often seen through campus riots and protests, led to a growing division between university administration and students. In July 1972, student demonstrations at the University of South Carolina planted a seed for the resurgence of the first-year seminar. After being barricaded in his office by student protesters, President Thomas F. Jones decided it was necessary "to develop a process to redo the first year and teach students to love the university" (Schroeder, 2003, p. 10). Under John Gardner's leadership (as director of the seminar at the University of South Carolina for more than three decades), foundational philosophies were established at South Carolina, which sparked a grassroots movement in the 1980s on other college and university campuses, allowing the first-year seminar to once again play a prominent role in students' college education.

The First-Year Seminar Today

Since the 1980s, first-year seminars have continued to grow in popularity while also evolving to meet the needs of college and university students. Gone are the days of the "traditional" college student. Today's college students are often considered the most diverse student population ever in American higher education (Debard, 2004). Instead of the typical 18- to 21-year-old student, 55% of college students are now 22 years of age or older (Chronicle of Higher Education, 2007). College students have also become more ethnically diverse. From 1994 to 2004, the percentage of African American students enrolled in higher education increased by 22.9%. Likewise, during the same time period, enrollment of Hispanic students increased by 22.6%, Asian Americans increased by 11.9%, and American Indians increased by 15.9% (Cook & Cordova, 2007).

As student diversity continues to grow, so do the needs of each incoming first-year class. Fortunately, "the structure of the first-year seminar is flexible enough to meet the growing needs of the changing student demographic" (Gahagan, 2002, p. 6). The seminar's adaptability to better address changing student needs is evidenced through the seminar survey findings, which since its first administration has reflected the diversity of seminar types and curriculum offered. The final chapter of this monograph provides some insight into how the seminar has changed.

Seminar Types

Betsy Barefoot and Paul Fidler (1992) identified five types of seminars based on the survey findings. This typology has changed very little since it was first introduced in the 1992 monograph. The five types are:

Extended Orientation Seminar. Sometimes called a freshman orientation, college survival, college transition, or student success course. Content likely will include introduction to campus resources, time management, academic and career planning, learning strategies, and an introduction to student development issues.

Academic seminar with generally uniform academic content across sections. May be an interdisciplinary or theme-oriented course, sometimes part of a general education requirement. Primary focus is on academic theme/discipline but will often include academic skills components such as critical thinking and expository writing.

Academic seminar on various topics. Similar to previously mentioned academic seminar except that specific topics vary from section to section.

Pre-professional or discipline-linked seminar. Designed to prepare students for the demands of the major/discipline and the profession. Generally taught within professional schools or specific disciplines such as engineering, health sciences, business, or education.

Basic study skills seminar. Offered for academically underprepared students. The focus is on basic academic skills such as grammar, notetaking, and reading texts.

In the 2006 survey administration, we added "hybrid seminar" to the above list, because over the past iterations it has been mentioned consistently as another type of seminar. It is defined as:

Hybrid. Has elements from two or more types of seminars.

Conclusion

This chapter provides an historical context for readers to consider as they review the most recent data on the characteristics, curricula, and practices drawn from the 2006 National Survey of First-Year Seminars. It is our hope that these findings continue to be valuable tools for administrators and faculty as we strive to improve the first-year seminar and the overall first-year experience for our students.

Notes

[1]The result of Gott v. Berea in 1913.

References

Barefoot, B. O., & Fidler, P. P. (1992). *1991 National Survey of Freshman Seminar Programming* (Monograph No. 10). Columbia, SC: University of South Carolina, National Resource Center for The Freshman Year Experience.

Barefoot, B. O., & Fidler, P. P. (1996). An historical and theoretical framework for the freshman seminar. *The 1994 national survey of freshman seminar programs: Continuing innovations in the collegiate curriculum.* (Monograph No. 20, pp. 5-9). Columbia, SC: University of South Carolina, National Resource Center for The Freshman Year Experience and Students in Transition.

Chronicle of Higher Education. (2007, August 1). *Almanac, 54*(1).

Cohen R. D., & Jody, R. (1978). *Freshman seminar: A new orientation.* Bolder, CO: Westview.

Cook, B. J., & Cordoba, D. I. (2007) *Minorities in higher education – The 22nd annual status report: 2007 supplement.* Washington, DC: American Council on Education.

Debard, R. (2004). Millennials coming to college. In M. D. Coomes & R. Debard (Eds.), *Serving the millennial generation* (New Directions in Student Services, No. 106, pp. 33-45). San Francisco: Jossey-Bass.

Drake, R. (1966). *Review of the literature for freshman orientation practices in the United States.* Fort Collins: Colorado State University.

Gahagan, J. S. (2002). A historical and theoretical framework for the first-year seminar: A brief history. *The 2000 National Survey of First-Year Seminar Programs: Continuing innovations in the collegiate curriculum* (Monograph No. 35, pp. 11-76). Columbia, SC: University of South Carolina, National Resource Center for The First-Year Experience and Students in Transition.

Gordon, V. N. (1989). Origins and purposes of the freshman seminar. In M. L. Upcraft & J. N. Gardner (Eds.), *The Freshman Year Experience* (pp. 183-197). San Francisco, CA: Jossey-Bass.

Mamrick, M. (2005). The first-year seminar: An historical perspective. In B. F. Tobolowsky, *The 2007 National Survey on First-Year Seminars: Continuing innovations in the collegiate curriculum* (Monograph No. 41, pp. 15-20). Columbia, SC: University of South Carolina, National Resource Center for The First-Year Experience and Students in Transition.

Schroeder, C. (2003). The first year and beyond: Charles Schroeder talks to John Gardner. *About Campus, 8*(2), 9-16.

Chapter 2

Methodology and Institutional Characteristics

Asheley Schryer, Angela Griffin, and Barbara F. Tobolowsky

This chapter provides details regarding the survey methodology, the profile of the institutions that participated in the survey, and a comparison between the percentage of participating institutions by affiliation, and the national percentages to determine the representativeness of the sample.

Methodology

The population for the 2006 National Survey was drawn from the electronic version of the 2007 *Higher Education Directory* (Burke, 2007)[1], which was released in October 2006. Institutions selected to receive an invitation to participate in the study had to be (a) regionally accredited, (b) not-for-profit, and (c) undergraduate-serving institutions.

The National Resource Center for The First-Year Experience and Students in Transition outsourced the administration of the survey instrument to Educational Benchmarking, Inc. (EBI). EBI was responsible for administering the survey via the Web, which included sending initial and follow-up e-mails that requested participation and providing the survey link and general data management.

The initial e-mail (sent November 18, 2006) served three primary functions: (a) notifying the recipient that the Center was conducting the seventh triennial survey "to gather information about the first-year seminars in American higher education," (b) providing information about the date the survey instrument would be sent, and (c) ensuring that the recipient was the appropriate contact for the survey, and if not, requesting the correct contact information. The initial e-mail was sent to chief academic officers (as listed in the *Higher Education Directory*) or the chief executive officer (as listed in the *Higher Education Directory*) if there was no chief academic officer listed in the directory. If the aforementioned positions were not included in the directory, the chief student affairs officer (as listed in the *Higher Education Directory*) was sent the e-mail. If none of these positions was listed in the directory, the institution was omitted from the study.

The initial respondents had approximately 10 days to reply with the replacement contact information before the next e-mail with the survey link was sent on November 28, 2006. Center staff or staff from EBI updated the database with the new contact information whenever a request was made. After applying the selection criteria and accounting for not verified (incorrect) or undeliverable (bounce backs) e-mails, the second e-mail with the survey link was sent to 2,646 potential participants.

All verified names in the database received reminder e-mails if they had not responded to the survey by December 5, 2006. Another reminder was sent to any verified recipients in the database who had not responded by December 12, 2006. In addition to sending the survey link, the reminder e-mails provided the deadline information (i.e., December 31, 2006). Although the plan was to end access to the survey by the end of the year, we decided to leave it open for an additional week to catch any late respondents. Thus, a "last chance" reminder e-mail was sent on January 5, 2007 reflecting the new date, and the survey closed officially on January 9, 2007.

Surveys were collected from 968 institutions (a 36.6% response rate). The respondents include 821 institutions (or 84.8%) offering a seminar and 147 institutions (15.2%) not offering a seminar. There were a small number of institutions that failed to reply to the question about whether or not they had a seminar. The responses of these institutions were reviewed and added to the database if they answered questions about the seminar or deleted if they did not. Since not answering the question could mean that they did not have a seminar or that they decided not to participate in the survey, they could not with any assurance be included in the list of institutions that did not have seminars. Chi-square analyses were conducted by type of seminar, institution affiliation (e.g., public/private), institution type (two-year/four-year), institution size, and selectivity.[2]

It should be noted that although this response rate is good for a web-based survey,[3] the relatively small number of respondents is a limitation. It is impossible to explain why individuals choose not to participate in a survey. However, some respondents expressed frustration with the language in the first e-mail, which may have affected this response rate. EBI referred to the contact information update request as a "survey." We heard from some potential participants who were confused when asked to respond to the "survey request" in the initial e-mail and then found a request for contact information and not the actual survey link. We suspect that the language might have caused such a degree of frustration in some potential respondents that they decided not to participate. Additionally, a handful of initial contacts, who did not provide us with a more appropriate recipient, complained about the number of reminders they received. This annoyance may have led them to choose not to participate as well. Nevertheless, although the response rate is far from ideal, it is an increase over the last administration (23.7% in 2003).[4]

Characteristics of Participating Institutions

Of the 968 institutions that responded to the survey, 821 offered first-year seminars. The 821 institutions serve as our sample for the analysis presented throughout this monograph. While the sample contains an approximately equal number of public and private schools, the majority of institutions are smaller, four-year schools. The tables that follow provide the demographic details. (See Tables 2.1-2.3.)

Table 2.1

Characteristics of Responding Institutions With Seminars (N = 821)

	Frequency	Percentage
Institutional type (n = 803)		
Two-year	188	23.4
Four-year	615	76.6
Institutional affiliation (n = 667)		
Private	351	52.6
Public	316	47.4
Institutional enrollment (n = 814)		
5,000 or less	553	67.9
5,001 - 10,000	129	15.8
10,001 - 15,000	61	7.5
15,001 - 20,000	35	4.3
More than 20,000	36	4.4

Note. Sample sizes vary based on survey responses.

Two-Year Institutions

Approximately 24% of respondents identified their institutions as two-year schools. The majority (91.9%) were public institutions. As Table 2.2 illustrates, these two-year institutions most often have 5,000 or fewer undergraduate students (60.1%).

Table 2.2

Undergraduate Headcount at Two-Year Institutions (n = 188)

Size of student body	Number of institutions	Percentage
5,000 or less	113	60.1
5,001 - 10,000	41	21.8
10,001 - 15,000	23	12.2
15,001 - 20,000	6	3.2
More than 20,000	5	2.7

Four-Year Institutions

Most survey respondents identified their institutions as four-year schools (76.7%), and the majority were private schools (63.2%). Like two-year institutions, most of the four-year institutions have 5,000 or fewer undergraduate students (71.1%). (See Table 2.3.)

Table 2.3
Undergraduate Headcount at Four-Year Institutions (n = 613)

Size of student body	Number of institutions	Percentage
5,000 or less	436	71.1
5,001 - 10,000	82	13.4
10,001 – 15,000	37	6.0
15,001 – 20,000	28	4.6
More than 20,000	30	4.9

Representation of 2006 Survey Respondents

Analyses were done to determine if the respondents were representative of accredited higher education institutions. There are significant statistical differences between all four institutional categories: (a) public two-year, (b) private two-year, (c) public four-year, and (d) private four-year. More specifically, these findings indicate that the survey sample under-represents two-year colleges. Conversely, the survey sample slightly over-represents private four-year institutions and greatly over-represents public four-year colleges and universities. Therefore, while it is not appropriate to draw firm generalizations from the data presented in the following chapters, that qualification does not diminish their value (See Table 2.4). The survey findings continue to be the most comprehensive portrait of the first-year seminar available, and, thus, provide valuable information to readers who hope to gather data to help them design, establish, and institutionalize the seminar on their campuses.

Table 2.4
Representation of 2006 Survey Respondents Compared to National Average by Institutional Type and Size (N = 654)

Type of institution	Number of institutions responding to survey[a]	Percentage	National percentage by type
Public two-year	114	17.4%*	32%
Private two-year	10	1.5%*	3%
Public four-year	195	30.0*	19%
Private four-year	335	51.2*	46%

Note. Figures for the national percentages are from the 2006 issue of *Almanac of the Chronicle of Higher Education* at chronicle.com/weekly/almanac/2006/nation.htm

[a]The survey totals listed include only those institutions that reported if they were public or private as well as a two-year or four-year institution. Incomplete answers were omitted from this total.

*$p < .05$

Notes

[1]The names in the 2007 electronic version were compared to the *2006 Higher Education Directory* available in hard copy. Institutions that were not in the 2006 directory (Burke, 2006), but were in the 2007 electronic directory, were omitted from the study for the purposes of consistency. Only United States institutions or those located in U.S. territories were included.

[2]Institutional representatives self-reported their selectivity, noted as "entrance difficulty level" on the survey, as high, moderate, and low. Those selecting moderate and low were grouped together in the analysis.

[3]Research (see Wang, Dziuban, & Moskal, 2001; Gunn, 2002) offers widely different accounts of the average response rate for web-based, e-mailed, and hard copy surveys. The response rate varies by sample, number of questions, topics, etc. For example, higher response rates are more likely with younger populations. It was very common to see web-based education surveys get approximately a 25% response rate.

[4]All the surveys prior to 2003 were paper surveys. The 2003 administration was the first web-based survey. The prior response rates for the seminar survey were: 53.6% in 1988, 43% in 1991, 40.7% in 1994, and 39.9% in 2000. Statistics are unavailable for 1997. The first web-based survey was conducted in 2003 and had a 23.7% response rate.

References

Burke, J. M. (Ed.). (2006). *2006 higher education directory*. Falls Church, VA: Higher Education Publications.

Burke, J. M. (Ed.). (2007). *2007 higher education directory*. Falls Church, VA: Higher Education Publications.

Gunn, H. (2002). *Web-based surveys: Changing the survey process.* Retrieved May 6, 2008, from http://www.firstmonday.org/issues/issue7_12/gunn/#g8

Wang, M. C., Dziuban, C. D., & Moskal, P. D. (2001). *A web-based survey system for distributed learning impact evaluation.* Retrieved May 6, 2008, from http://www.scinecedirect.com/science?_ob=ArticleURL&_udi=B6W4X-4…urlVersion=0&_userid=521354&md5=33e1992e6dcfe0b2ab4e4402fc3f132

Chapter 3

The First-Year Seminar Characteristics

Angela Griffin, Jonathan Romm, and Barbara F. Tobolowsky

This chapter describes the curricular details of the course including longevity, seminar type, credit hours, course content, and administration. It concludes with a listing of successful or innovative course components as reported by survey respondents. When applicable, data for each topic are reported across all institutions and by institutional type and affiliation, size, selectivity, and seminar type. In some instances, survey questions required open-ended responses, and those narratives are included in this chapter as well.

Course Longevity

The majority of institutions reported that their seminars were at least three years old, and nearly half indicated that their seminars were more than 10 years old. More than one third of two-year institutions reported that they have offered their first-year seminar for more than 10 years, and about half of two-year institutions have offered their first-year seminar for three to 10 years (48.9%). Similar to the two-year institutions, the majority of four-year institutions have offered first-year seminars for three years or more. More than 40% have offered seminars for three to 10 years, but 51.9% have offered them for more than 10 years (Tables 3.1-3.6).

Table 3.1
Seminar Longevity Across All Institutions (*N* = 810)

Longevity	Frequency	Percentage
Two years or less	79	9.8
Three to 10 years	344	42.5
More than 10 years	387	47.8

Table 3.2
Seminar Longevity by Institutional Affiliation (*N* = 65)

Longevity	Private (*n* = 346)	Public (*n* = 313)
Two years or less	6.1%	9.9%
Three to 10 years*	39.9%	48.2%
More than 10 years**	54.1%	41.9 %

*p < .05. **p < .01.

Table 3.3
Seminar Longevity by Institutional Type (*N* = 797)

Longevity	Two-year (*n* = 184)	Four-year (*n* = 613)
Two years or less**	17.4%	7.5%
Three to 10 years*	48.9%	40.6%
More than 10 years**	33.7%	51.9%

*p < .05. **p < .01.

Table 3.4
Seminar Longevity by Institutional Selectivity (*N* = 810)

Longevity	High (*n* = 115)	Other (*n* = 695)
Two years or less*	3.5%	10.8%
Three to 10 years*	32.2%	44.2%
More than 10 years**	64.4%	45.0%

*p < .05. **p < .01.

Table 3.5
Seminar Longevity by Institutional Size (*N* = 810)

Longevity	5,000 or less (*n* = 553)	5,001 - 10,000 (*n* = 127)	10,001 - 15,000 (*n* = 60)	15,001 - 20,000 (*n* = 34)	More than 20,000 (*n* = 36)
Two years or less	9.6%	15.0%	10.0%	2.9%	0.0%
Three to 10 years	43.2%	44.9%	30.0%	55.9%	30.6%
More than 10 years	47.2%	40.2%	60.0%	41.2%	69.4%

p < .05

Table 3.6

Seminar Longevity by Seminar Type (*N* = 765)

Longevity	EO (*n* = 314)	AUC (*n* = 134)	AVC (*n* = 138)	BSS (*n* = 42)	PRE (*n* = 11)	Hybrid (*n* = 124)
Two years or less	9.9%	9.7%	7.3%	4.8%	18.2%	12.9%
Three to 10 years	45.9%	38.8%	41.3%	52.4%	36.4%	33.9%
More than 10 years	44.3%	51.5%	51.5%	42.9%	45.5%	53.2%

Note. When *n* for seminar type <10, data were omitted from table. EO = extended orientation seminar, AUC = academic seminar with uniform content, AVC = academic seminar with variable content, BSS = basic study skills seminar, PRE = pre-professional or discipline seminar.

Types of Seminars Offered

Since the initial survey administration, respondents have been asked to indicate the types of first-year seminars offered on their campuses. In 1991, the National Resource Center identified five discrete seminar types plus an "other" option from which institutional representatives could select (see chapter 2 for definitions). Over the years, a number of participants selected the "other" option and described their course as a "hybrid." In the 2006 administration, we attempted to tease out the specific differences between a "hybrid" (has "elements from two or more types of seminars") course and "other." Therefore, in this administration, respondents could choose between six seminar types and the "other" option.

The majority of institutions (57.9%) noted that they offered an extended orientation seminar. Academic seminars, both those with uniform content (28.1%) and variable content across sections (25.7%), were each offered by approximately one quarter of the responding institutions. A number of institutions also indicated that they offered basic study skills seminars (21.6%). A significant number of institutions reported that they offered more than one type of first-year seminar (Table 3.7).

Of the responding institutions, 20.3% noted that their courses fell in the hybrid category versus 4.4% that were characterized as "other." As follow-up questions, we asked for a description of the hybrid course and the "other" option. Hybrids were most frequently combinations of an extended orientation course and an academic seminar with uniform content, which reflects an overall trend toward an increase in academic seminars. (See chapter 6 for additional discussion of trends.)

Those institutions that selected the "other" response reported offering a range of courses. Many of these courses were characterized as being yearlong (University of California, Los Angeles), interdisciplinary (UCLA, Duke), focused on topics of current interest (UCLA, Duke), focused on career exploration (North Hennepin Community College, James Madison University), and/or leadership development (Hope International University). At UCLA, the yearlong courses had an unusual structure that included larger lectures with small discussion sections. Duke University offered interdisciplinary clusters in which students took at least two seminars that addressed similar themes but from different disciplines. Other courses were designed for specific student populations. For example, Lyme Academy College of Fine Arts offered seminars that were uniquely valuable for their art students, such as "How to Frame Your Art" and "How to Take Digital Images." As these examples illustrate, there is a lot of variability in the range of courses identified as "other" and hybrid.

When seminar type was examined by institutional affiliation (public, private), institutional type (two-year, four-year), and admissions selectivity, a number of other differences emerged. Extended orientation and basic study skills seminars were more frequently offered in public and two-year institutions, and institutions that were not highly selective, whereas academic seminars, both with uniform and variable content across sections, were more frequent in private and four-year institutions. Furthermore, academic seminars with variable content across sections were more prevalent at highly selective institutions. Finally, hybrids were more common at four-year institutions (Tables 3.8-3.11).

Table 3.7
Respondents Offering Each Type of Seminar Across All Institutions (N = 821)

Seminar type	Frequency	Percentage
Extended orientation	475	57.9
Academic (uniform content)	231	28.1
Academic (variable content)	211	25.7
Basic study skills	177	21.6
Pre-professional or discipline-linked	122	14.9
Hybrid	167	20.3
Other	36	4.4

Note. Percentages do not equal 100%. Respondents could make more than one selection.

Table 3.8
Percentage of Respondents Offering Each Type of Seminar by Institutional Affiliation (N = 667)

Seminar type	Private (n = 351)	Public (n = 316)
Extended orientation**	49.6	67.4
Academic (uniform content)*	31.3	23.1
Academic (variable content)*	29.3	21.2
Basic study skills**	13.1	26.6
Pre-professional**	8.6	21.5
Hybrid	21.4	18.7
Other	4.3	4.8

Note. Percentages do not equal 100%. Respondents could make more than one selection.
*p < .05. **p < .01.

Table 3.9

Percentage of Respondents Offering Each Type of Seminar by Institutional Type (N = 807)

Seminar type	Two-year (*n* = 188)	Four-year (*n* = 619)
Extended orientation**	77.1	51.5
Academic (uniform content)*	21.8	29.9
Academic (variable content)**	6.9	31.5
Basic study skills**	41.0	15.7
Pre-professional	12.2	15.2
Hybrid**	12.8	23.1
Other	2.1	5.0

Note. Percentages do not equal 100%. Respondents could make more than one selection.
*p < .05. **p < .01.

Table 3.10

Percentage of Respondents Offering Each Type of Seminar by Institutional Selectivity (N = 821)

Seminar type	High (*n* = 117)	Other (*n* = 704)
Extended orientation**	33.3	61.9
Academic (uniform content)	29.1	28.0
Academic (variable content)**	60.7	19.9
Basic study skills**	8.6	23.7
Pre-professional	12.0	15.3
Hybrid	16.2	21.0
Other	7.7	3.8

Note. Percentages do not equal 100%. Respondents could make more than one selection.
**p < .01

Table 3.11
Percentage of Respondents Offering Each Type of Seminar by Institutional Size (N = 821)

Seminar type	5,000 or less (*n* = 560)	5,001-10,000 (*n* = 129)	10,001-15,000 (*n* = 61)	15,001-20,000 (*n* = 35)	More than 20,000 (*n* = 36)
Extended orientation*	54.3	61.2	70.5	60.0	77.8
Academic (uniform content)	28.8	27.9	26.2	22.9	27.8
Academic (variable content)*	25.2	24.0	23.0	22.9	47.2
Basic study skills	19.5	25.6	26.2	25.7	27.8
Pre-professional*	9.6	24.0	27.9	34.3	22.2
Hybrid	20.5	23.3	16.4	20.0	13.9
Other*	3.9	4.7	0.0	11.4	11.1

Note. Percentages do not equal 100%. Respondents could make more than one selection.
*$p < .05$

Primary Seminar Types

While the majority of institutions reported that they offered more than one type of seminar, survey respondents were asked to complete the survey based on the seminar type with the highest total enrollment. The extended orientation seminar was most frequently cited as having the highest enrollment across all institutions. However, a comparison by institutional type showed that public institutions reported higher enrollments for extended orientation and basic study skills seminars, while private and four-year institutions reported higher enrollments for academic seminars of both uniform and variable content. Two-year institutions were more likely to offer extended orientation and basic study stills seminars than four-year institutions (Tables 3.12-3.16).

Table 3.12
Respondents' Primary Seminar Type Across All Institutions (N = 772)

Seminar type	Frequency	Percentage
Extended orientation	316	40.9
Academic (uniform content)	134	17.4
Academic (variable content)	138	17.9
Basic study skills	45	5.8
Pre-professional	12	1.6
Hybrid	125	16.2
Other	2	0.3

Table 3.13

Percentage of Respondents Reporting Primary Seminar Type by Institutional Affiliation (N = 633)

Seminar type	Private (*n* = 328)	Public (*n* = 305)
Extended orientation**	32.9	51.2
Academic (uniform content)*	20.7	13.8
Academic (variable content)**	24.1	11.5
Basic study skills **	2.1	7.2
Pre-professional	0.9	1.6
Hybrid	18.9	14.4
Other	0.3	0.3

*$p < .05$. **$p < .01$.

Table 3.14

Percentage of Respondents Reporting Primary Seminar Type by Institutional Type (N = 760)

Seminar type	Two-year (*n* = 180)	Four-year (*n* = 580)
Extended orientation**	59.4	34.8
Academic (uniform content)*	11.1	19.1
Academic (variable content)**	1.7	23.1
Basic study skills**	18.3	1.9
Pre-professional	0.0	2.1
Hybrid**	9.4	18.6
Other	0.0	0.3

*$p < .05$. **$p < .01$.

Table 3.15

Percentage of Respondents Reporting Primary Seminar Type by Institutional Selectivity (N = 772)

Seminar type	High (*n* = 114)	Other (*n* = 658)
Extended orientation**	14.0	45.6
Academic (uniform content)	15.8	17.6
Academic (variable content)**	54.4	11.6
Basic study skills*	0.9	6.7
Pre-professional	0.9	1.7
Hybrid	13.2	16.7
Other	0.9	0.2

* $p < .05$. **$p < .01$.

Table 3.16
Percentage of Respondents Reporting Primary Seminar Type by Institutional Size (N = 772)

Seminar type	5,000 or less (*n* = 520)	5,001-10,000 (*n* = 125)	10,001-15,000 (*n* = 58)	15,001-20,000 (*n* = 34)	More than 20,000 (*n* = 35)
Extended orientation (EO)	38.9	40.8	55.2	52.9	37.2
Academic (uniform content)(AUC)	18.9	16.0	13.8	5.9	17.1
Academic (variable content) (AVC)	18.7	17.6	8.6	8.8	31.4
Basic study skills (BSS)	5.0	8.0	8.6	5.9	5.7
Pre-professional (PRE)	1.5	1.6	3.5	0.0	0.0
Hybrid	17.1	16.0	10.3	26.5	2.9
Other	0.0	0.0	0.0	0.0	5.7

p < .05

Online Components

In 2003, we discovered that approximately 13% of responding institutions offered part or all their first-year seminars online. Almost 5% offered at least one section of their seminar totally online. In 2006, 49% of participating institutions offered at least some online component, and 11.6% offered online-only sections. A larger proportion of public institutions reported the use of online course components as compared to private institutions (56.8% vs. 43.8%). Also, more hybrid courses had online components (54.5%) than other seminar types (Tables 3.17-3.28).

Institutions that provided details regarding their use of online components tended to mention using course management software, such as Blackboard or WebCT. Other participating institutions indicated that career assessments (Arkansas Northeastern College), developmental math programs (University of Arkansas Community College of Hope), or some course topics (e.g., learning styles, time management, career planning, and financial management at McHenry County College) were offered online. Certainly, the most common uses of online components were for conducting discussions, e-mailing students, posting assignments, turning in papers, taking quizzes, and providing the course syllabus.

Some of the more current technological developments were reflected in the details some institutions provided as well. For example, one institution mentioned using wikis (Ottawa University), another listed podcasts (College of Mount St. Joseph), and a few mentioned using class blogs (Lasell College). This growing use of technology seems to reflect the developments in the technology field. In other words, as technology develops new options, higher education will make use of those technological advances.

Table 3.17
Online-Only Seminar Sections Across All Institutions (*N*= 791)

	Yes	**No**
Frequency	92	699
Percentage	11.6	88.4

Table 3.18
Online-Only Seminar Sections by Institutional Affiliation (*N* = 641)

	Private (***n* = 337**)	**Public** (***n* = 304**)
Frequency	13	53
Percentage	3.9	17.4

p < .05

Table 3.19
Online-Only Seminar Sections by Institutional Type (*N* = 777)

	Two-year (***n* = 185**)	**Four-year** (***n* = 592**)
Frequency	58	31
Percentage	31.4	5.2

p < .05

Table 3.20
Online-Only Seminar Sections by Institutional Selectivity (*N* = 791)

	High (***n* = 106**)	**Other** (***n* = 685**)
Frequency	2	90
Percentage	1.9	13.1

p < .05

Table 3.21
Online-Only Seminar Sections by Institutional Size (*N* = 791)

	5,000 or less (***n* = 542**)	**5,001 - 10,000** (***n* = 124**)	**10,001 - 15,000** (***n* = 58**)	**15,001 - 20,000** (***n* = 32**)	**More than 20,000** (***n* = 35**)
Frequency	44	28	9	5	6
Percentage	8.1	22.6	15.5	15.6	17.1

p < .05

Table 3.22
Online-Only Seminar Sections by Seminar Type (N = 747)

	EO (*n* = 307)	AUC (*n* = 130)	AVC (*n* = 131)	BSS (*n* = 43)	PRE (*n* = 11)	Hybrid (*n* = 123)
Frequency	50	14	2	11	1	10
Percentage	16.3	10.8	1.5	25.6	9.1	8.1

Note. When *n* for seminar type <10, data were omitted from table.
$p < .05$

Table 3.23
Seminar Includes Online Components Across All Institutions (N = 795)

	Yes	No
Frequency	390	405
Percentage	49.1	50.9

Table 3.24
Seminar Includes Online Components by Institutional Affiliation (N = 643)

	Private (*n* = 340)	Public (*n* = 303)
Frequency	149	172
Percentage	43.8	56.8

$p < .05$

Table 3.25
Seminar Includes Online Components by Institutional Type (N = 781)

	Two-year (*n* = 184)	Four-year (*n* = 597)
Frequency	97	286
Percentage	52.7	47.9

Table 3.26
Seminar Includes Online Components by Institutional Selectivity (N = 795)

	High (*n* = 108)	Other (*n* = 687)
Frequency	51	339
Percentage	47.2	49.3

Table 3.27
Seminar Includes Online Components by Institutional Size (N = 795)

	5,000 or less (*n* = 546)	5,001 - 10,000 (*n* = 123)	10,001 - 15,000 (*n* = 59)	15,001 - 20,000 (*n* = 33)	More than 20,000 (*n* = 34)
Frequency	247	80	29	18	16
Percentage	45.2	65.0	49.2	54.6	47.1

p < .05

Table 3.28
Seminar Includes Online Components by Seminar Type (N = 749)

	EO (*n* = 306)	AUC (*n* = 132)	AVC (*n* = 132)	BSS (*n* = 43)	PRE (*n* = 12)	Hybrid (*n* = 123)
Frequency	152	65	67	17	4	67
Percentage	49.7	49.6	50.8	39.5	33.3	54.5

Note. When *n* for seminar type <10, data were omitted from table.

Seminars Embedded in Learning Communities

In 2003, the survey asked respondents if "any sections linked one or more courses (i.e., learning community—enrolling a cohort of students into two or more courses)." Approximately 25% of the institutions said they did offer linked courses and were invited to describe those courses in that survey administration. We posed the same set of questions in 2006 and found that 35.3% of the responding institutions offered linked courses (Tables 3.29-3.34). Almost all of the participating institutions provided some details about their course linkages. The most striking finding, though hardly surprising, is that the course links and structures varied greatly. The most common linkages mentioned were between the seminar and English, math, science, or a general education course (which was sometimes identified as psychology, philosophy, art, history, or music). Some participating institutions created learning communities that were organized by theme. For example, Fort Lewis College identified 20 different communities, from those for art majors and biology majors to learning communities on the "Nature of Business" and "Craft of Research."

Some responding institutions did not provide specific information regarding the course linkages but did discuss the structure of their learning communities more broadly. For instance, some institutions linked two courses (Gateway Community College, John Jay College of Criminal Justice, CUNY), but others mentioned that the linkages were among three or four courses (Indiana University East). At UC Berkeley, the links were tied to theme floors in the residence halls. For example, Global Environment was one such theme, and only students in that hall could enroll in the course. Some of the learning communities were tied to developmental courses (Elgin Community College), but others were for honors students (Indiana Wesleyan University, Simmons College). Though the structure may initially be a challenge for campuses to institute, the wide range of forms and increasing numbers of learning communities that include a first-year seminar suggest they have become a popular curricular innovation.

Table 3.29
Seminar Is Part of Learning Community Across All Institutions (*N* = 794)

	Yes	**No**
Frequency	280	514
Percentage	35.3	64.7

Table 3.30
Seminar Is Part of Learning Community by Institutional Affiliation (*N* = 644)

	Private **(*n* = 339)**	**Public** **(*n* = 305)**
Frequency	94	141
Percentage	27.7	46.2

p < .05

Table 3.31
Seminar Is Part of Learning Community by Institutional Type (*N* = 780)

	Two-year **(*n* = 182)**	**Four-year** **(*n* = 598)**
Frequency	56	219
Percentage	30.8	36.6

Table 3.32
Seminar Is Part of Learning Community by Institutional Selectivity (*N* = 794)

	High **(*n* = 110)**	**Other** **(*n* = 684)**
Frequency	32	248
Percentage	29.1	36.3

Table 3.33
Seminar is Part of Learning Community by Institutional Size (*N* = 794)

	5,000 or less **(*n* = 544)**	**5,001 - 10,000** **(*n* = 123)**	**10,001 - 15,000** **(*n* = 58)**	**15,001 - 20,000** **(*n* = 33)**	**More than 20,000** **(*n* = 36)**
Frequency	152	56	29	24	19
Percentage	27.9	45.5	50.0	72.7	52.8

p < .05

Table 3.34

Seminar Is Part of Learning Community by Seminar Type (*N* = 749)

	EO (*n* = 307)	AUC (*n* = 129)	AVC (*n* = 135)	BSS (*n* = 44)	PRE (*n* = 12)	Hybrid (*n* = 120)
Frequency	112	48	41	12	5	47
Percentage	36.5	37.2	30.4	27.3	41.7	39.2

Note. When *n* for seminar type <10, data were omitted from table.

Service-Learning Component

We asked about the use of a service-learning component in any section of the seminar[1] for the first time on the 2003 survey instrument. That year, almost a quarter of the respondents (22.7%) offered a service-learning component. In the 2006 administration, 40.2% of responding institutions said that they offered a service-learning component, with private institutions more likely to offer service-learning than public institutions (51.5% vs. 31.5%) (Tables 3.35-3.40).

Although some participants stated the service-learning activity was required, most said that it was optional. The activity varied from a half-day (Peace College) or day (Regis College, Cal Polytechnic State University, Rollins College, Franklin College) of service to a 32-hour requirement (Albany State University). Emory and Henry College had students participate in a "Service Plunge," which was a half-day of service that took place on the first Saturday after classes began. The "Plunge" scheduling suggests that the service-learning activity might be offered as a special event for first-year students as the common reading program is on some campuses.

The type of service activities mentioned by participants ranged from working with area nonprofit organizations (Emerson College) to tutoring low-income elementary school students (Concordia University). A number of institutions mentioned teaming with Habitat for Humanity (University of Nebraska-Kearney, Southwest Missouri State University) as well. At Tusculum College, service-learning is an integral part of their mission. The college offers a service-learning course that is required for graduation, in addition to the service-learning component in the first-year seminar. The range of activities and time commitments mentioned reflect the varying institutional approaches to service-learning. Yet, the increase in the number of responding institutions who provide service-learning activities (required or optional) may be indicative that a greater value is being placed on this component.

Table 3.35

Seminar Includes Service-Learning Component Across All Institutions (*N* = 801)

	Yes	No
Frequency	322	479
Percentage	40.2	59.8

Table 3.36
Seminar Includes Service-Learning Component by Institutional Affiliation ($N = 650$)

	Private ($n = 342$)	Public ($n = 308$)
Frequency	176	97
Percentage	51.5	31.5

$p < .05$

Table 3.37
Seminar Includes Service-Learning Component by Institutional Type ($N = 787$)

	Two-year ($n = 184$)	Four-year ($n = 603$)
Frequency	25	293
Percentage	13.6	48.6

$p < .05$

Table 3.38
Seminar Includes Service-Learning Component by Institutional Selectivity ($N = 801$)

	High ($n = 111$)	Other ($n = 690$)
Frequency	49	273
Percentage	44.1	39.6

Table 3.39
Seminar Includes Service-Learning Component by Institutional Size ($N = 801$)

	5,000 or less ($n = 551$)	5,001 - 10,000 ($n = 124$)	10,001 - 15,000 ($n = 58$)	15,001 - 20,000 ($n = 32$)	More than 20,000 ($n = 36$)
Frequency	234	40	19	16	13
Percentage	42.5	32.3	32.8	50.0	36.1

Table 3.40
Seminar Includes Service-Learning Component by Seminar Type ($N = 755$)

	EO ($n = 309$)	AUC ($n = 130$)	AVC ($n = 137$)	BSS ($n = 42$)	PRE ($n = 12$)	Hybrid ($n = 123$)
Frequency	97	59	76	4	6	55
Percentage	31.4	45.4	55.5	9.5	50.0	44.7

Note. When *n* for seminar type <10, data were omitted from table.
$p < .05$.

Class Size

The majority of institutions reported that their seminars had approximate class sizes of either 16 to 20 students (36.9%) or 21 to 25 students (29.8%). Private and highly selective institutions were more likely to have class sizes of 20 or fewer students. At two-year institutions, 35.8% of the sections had between 21 and 25 students, and 27.3% had 16 to 20 students. Four-year institutions reported that most of their seminar sections enrolled between 21 and 25 students (27.8%) or 16 to 20 students (40.3%) (Tables 3.41-3.46).

Table 3.41

Percentage of Respondents Reporting Approximate Class Size Across All Institutions (N = 808)

Class size	Frequency	Percentage
Under 10	6	0.7
10 - 15	147	18.2
16 - 20	298	36.9
21 - 25	241	29.8
26 - 30	61	7.6
Over 30	55	6.8

Table 3.42

Percentage of Respondents Reporting Approximate Class Size by Institutional Affiliation (N = 657)

Class size	Private (*n* = 345)	Public (*n* = 312)
Under 10	1.2	0.0
10 - 15**	26.7	11.2
16 - 20**	44.1	27.6
21 - 25**	19.4	41.7
26 - 30**	3.5	9.9
Over 30*	5.2	9.6

*$p < .05$. **$p < .01$.

Table 3.43
Percentage of Respondents Reporting Approximate Class Size by Institutional Type (*N* = 795)

Class size	Two-year (*n* = 187)	Four-year (*n* = 608)
Under 10	1.1	0.7
10 - 15	15.5	19.1
16 - 20**	27.3	40.3
21 - 25*	35.8	27.8
26 - 30*	11.7	6.1
Over 30	8.6	6.1

*$p < .05$. **$p < .01$.

Table 3.44
Percentage of Respondents Reporting Approximate Class Size by Institutional Selectivity (*N* = 808)

Class size	High (*n* = 113)	Other (*n* = 695)
Under 10	1.8	0.6
10 - 15*	27.4	16.7
16 - 20**	53.1	34.2
21 - 25**	11.5	32.8
26 - 30*	1.8	8.5
Over 30	4.4	7.2

*$p < .05$. **$p < .01$.

Table 3.45
Percentage of Respondents Reporting Approximate Class Size by Institutional Size (*N* = 808)

Class size	5,000 or less (*n* = 552)	5,001 - 10,000 (*n* = 126)	10,001 - 15,000 (*n* = 60)	15,001 - 20,000 (*n* = 34)	More than 20,000 (*n* = 36)
Under 10	1.1	0.0	0.0	0.0	0.0
10 - 15	22.3	11.9	8.3	2.9	8.3
16 - 20	41.5	31.0	20.0	20.6	30.6
21 - 25	22.5	42.1	51.7	58.8	36.1
26 - 30	5.8	7.9	10.0	14.7	22.2
Over 30	6.9	7.1	10.0	2.9	2.8

$p < .05$

Table 3.46

Percentage of Respondents Reporting Approximate Class Size by Seminar Type (N = 763)

Class size	EO (*n* = 314)	AUC (*n* = 132)	AVC (*n* = 138)	BSS (*n* = 44)	PRE (*n* = 12)	Hybrid (*n* = 121)
Under 10	0.3	0.8	0.0	4.6	0.0	0.8
10 - 15*	13.1	16.7	30.4	27.3	8.3	14.9
16 - 20*	28.0	43.2	52.2	22.7	58.3	38.8
21 - 25*	37.9	22.7	12.3	36.4	16.7	36.4
26 - 30*	10.2	9.1	2.2	9.1	8.3	6.6
Over 30*	10.5	7.6	2.9	0.0	8.3	2.5

Note. When *n* for seminar type <10, data were omitted from table.

*$p < .05$

Seminar Length

Across all participating institutions, the seminar was typically one semester long. This is true at both two- and four-year institutions (76.3% and 76.1%, respectively). The next most common seminar length was one quarter for two-year institutions (12.4%) and one year at four-year institutions (10.1%) (Table 3.47-3.52).

Table 3.47

Seminar Length Across All Institutions (N = 804)

Course duration	Frequency	Percentage
One semester	611	76.0
One year	65	8.1
One quarter	50	6.2
Other	78	9.7

Table 3.48

Seminar Length by Institutional Affiliation (N = 652)

Course duration	Private (*n* = 343)	Public (*n* = 309)
One semester	73.2%	78.6%
One year**	11.7%	4.2%
One quarter*	4.4%	9.4%
Other	10.8%	7.8%

*$p < .05$. **$p < .01$.

Table 3.49
Seminar Length by Institutional Type (*N* = 792)

Course duration	Two-year (*n* = 186)	Four-year (*n* = 606)
One semester	76.3%	76.1%
One year**	2.2%	10.1%
One quarter**	12.4%	4.1%
Other	9.1%	9.7%

**p < .01

Table 3.50
Seminar Length by Institutional Selectivity (*N* = 804)

Course duration	High (*n* = 114)	Other (*n* = 690)
One semester**	64.9%	77.8%
One year	12.3%	7.4%
One quarter	8.8%	5.8%
Other	14.0%	9.0%

**p < .01

Table 3.51
Seminar Length by Institutional Size (*N* = 804)

Course duration	5,000 or less (*n* = 551)	5,001 - 10,000 (*n* = 127)	10,001 - 15,000 (*n* = 59)	15,001 - 20,000 (*n* = 32)	More than 20,000 (*n* = 35)
One semester	74.6%	76.4%	83.1%	87.5%	74.3%
One year	9.4 %	7.1%	5.1%	0.0%	2.9%
One quarter	5.6%	3.9%	6.8%	9.4%	20.0%
Other	10.3%	12.6%	5.1%	3.1%	2.9%

p < .05

Table 3.52

Seminar Length by Seminar Type (N = 758)

Course duration	EO (n = 308)	AUC (n = 132)	AVC (n = 138)	BSS (n = 44)	PRE (n = 12)	Hybrid (n = 122)
One semester	75.3%	67.4%	80.4%	81.8%	91.7%	78.7%
One year	4.2%	17.4%	7.3%	4.6%	8.3%	8.2%
One quarter	8.4%	6.1%	4.4%	9.1%	0.0%	3.3%
Other	12.0%	9.1%	8.0%	4.6%	0.0%	9.8%

Note. When *n* for seminar type <10, data were omitted from table.

$p < .05$

Seminar as Required Course

Almost half (46%) of the responding institutions required all of their first-year students to take the first-year seminar. On the other hand, nearly 20% of institutions reported that the course was not required for any student. Private schools were more likely than public schools to require the course for all first-year students (66.5% vs. 25.9%, respectively). A larger number of four-year institutions required all of their first-year students to take their seminar than two-year institutions (54.2% vs. 19.7%). Institutions that were not highly selective were more likely to require provisionally admitted students to take the first-year seminar than schools that were highly selective (Tables 3.53-3.64).

Table 3.53

Percentage of First-Year Students Required to Take Seminar Across All Institutions (N = 804)

Percentage of students required to take seminar	Frequency	Percentage
100%	370	46.0
90 - 99%	73	9.1
80 - 89%	26	3.2
70 - 79%	19	2.4
60 - 69%	10	1.2
50 - 59%	19	2.4
Less than 50%	131	16.3
0%	156	19.4

Table 3.54

Percentage of First-Year Students Required to Take Seminar by Institutional Affiliation (*N* = 655)

Percentage of students required to take seminar	Private (*n* = 346)	Public (*n* = 309)
100%**	66.5	25.9
90 - 99%*	11.9	6.5
80 - 89%	2.6	4.5
70 - 79%	2.3	1.9
60 - 69%	0.6	1.3
50 - 59%	1.7	2.6
Less than 50%**	4.6	27.2
0%**	9.8	30.1

*p < .05. ***p* < .01.

Table 3.55

Percentage of First-Year Students Required to Take Seminar by Institutional Type (*N* = 790)

Percentage of students required to take seminar	Two-year (*n* = 183)	Four-year (*n* = 607)
100%**	19.7	54.2
90 - 99%	8.2	9.6
80 - 89%*	6.6	2.3
70 - 79%	4.4	1.8
60 - 69%	2.7	0.8
50 - 59%	3.8	2.0
Less than 50%**	23.5	13.7
0%**	31.2	15.7

*p < .05. ***p* < .01.

Table 3.56

Percentage of First-Year Students Required to Take Seminar by Institutional Selectivity ($N = 804$)

Percentage of students required to take seminar	High ($n = 113$)	Other ($n = 691$)
100%**	62.8	43.3
90 - 99%**	1.8	10.3
80 - 89%	0.0	3.8
70 - 79%	1.8	2.5
60 - 69%	0.0	1.5
50 - 59%	0.9	2.6
Less than 50%**	5.3	18.1
0%*	27.4	18.1

*$p < .05$. **$p < .01$.

Table 3.57

Percentage of First-Year Students Required to Take Seminar by Institutional Size ($N = 804$)

Percentage of students required to take seminar	5,000 or less ($n = 550$)	5,001 - 10,000 ($n = 126$)	10,001 - 15,000 ($n = 59$)	15,001 - 20,000 ($n = 34$)	More than 20,000 ($n = 35$)
100%	57.5	28.6	20.3	5.9	11.4
90 - 99%	10.6	7.2	5.1	5.9	2.9
80 - 89%	4.0	1.6	1.7	2.9	0.0
70 - 79%	2.5	3.2	0.0	2.9	0.0
60 - 69%	1.1	0.0	5.1	2.9	0.0
50 - 59%	1.6	4.0	5.1	2.9	2.9
Less than 50%	9.5	26.2	40.7	29.4	34.3
0%	13.3	29.4	22.0	47.1	48.6

$p < .05$

Table 3.58

Percentage of First-Year Students Required to Take Seminar by Seminar Type (*N* = 759)

Percentage of students required to take seminar	EO (*n* = 312)	AUC (*n* = 132)	AVC (*n* = 136)	BSS (*n* = 44)	PRE (*n* = 12)	Hybrid (*n* = 121)
100%	36.9	62.1	58.1	4.6	41.7	47.1
90 - 99%	11.5	9.9	5.2	0.0	8.3	11.6
80 - 89%	4.2	2.3	1.5	6.8	8.3	1.7
70 - 79%	3.2	1.5	1.5	0.0	0.0	2.5
60 - 69%	1.0	1.5	0.7	2.3	8.3	1.7
50 - 59%	2.9	0.8	1.5	6.8	0.0	3.3
Less than 50%	21.2	10.6	4.4	40.9	33.3	16.5
0%	19.2	11.4	27.2	38.6	0.0	15.7

Note. When *n* for seminar type <10, data were omitted from table.

p < .05

Table 3.59

Type of Students Required to Take Seminar Across All Institutions (*N* = 821)

Students required to take seminar	Frequency	Percentage
Provisionally admitted students	165	20.1
Undeclared students	136	16.6
Student athletes	136	16.6
Honors students	133	16.2
Students in specific majors	131	16.0
Learning community participants	121	14.7
Other	388	47.3
None	169	20.6

Note. Percentages do not equal 100%. Respondents could make more than one selection.

Table 3.60

Type of Students Required to Take Seminar by Institutional Affiliation (N = 667)

Students required to take seminar	Private (*n* = 351)	Public (*n* = 316)
Provisionally admitted students	20.5%	19.3%
Undeclared students**	22.2%	10.1%
Student athletes**	20.8%	11.7%
Honors students**	20.8%	11.4%
Students in specific majors	16.8%	14.9%
Learning community participants	16.0%	13.6%
Other**	59.3%	35.8%
None**	10.0%	31.3%

Note. Percentages do not equal 100%. Respondents could make more than one selection.
**$p < .01$

Table 3.61

Type of Students Required to Take Seminar by Institutional Type (N = 807)

Students required to take seminar	Two-year (*n* = 188)	Four-year (*n* = 619)
Provisionally admitted students**	12.2%	22.6%
Undeclared students**	4.8%	20.2%
Student athletes**	5.3%	20.0%
Honors students**	4.3%	20.0%
Students in specific majors*	9.6%	17.8%
Learning community participants**	7.5%	17.1%
Other	42.0%	49.1%
None**	33.5%	16.5%

Note. Percentages do not equal 100%. Respondents could make more than one selection.
*$p < .05$. **$p < .01$.

Table 3.62
Type of Students Required to Take Seminar by Institutional Selectivity (*N* = 821)

Students required to take seminar	High (*n* = 117)	Other (*n* = 704)
Provisionally admitted students*	12.0%	21.5%
Undeclared students	14.5%	16.9%
Student athletes	17.1%	16.5%
Honors students	18.0%	15.9%
Students in specific majors	16.2%	15.9%
Learning community participants	14.5%	14.8%
Other	46.2%	47.4%
None	27.4%	19.5%

Note. Percentages do not equal 100%. Respondents could make more than one selection.
*$p < .05$

Table 3.63
Type of Students Required to Take Seminar by Institutional Size (*N* = 821)

Students required to take seminar	5,000 or less (*n* = 560)	5,001 - 10,000 (*n* = 129)	10,001 - 15,000 (*n* = 61)	15,001 - 20,000 (*n* = 35)	More than 20,000 (*n* = 36)
Provisionally admitted students	20.4%	20.9%	21.3%	11.4%	19.4%
Undeclared students*	19.6%	10.9%	13.1%	5.7%	5.6%
Student athletes	17.5%	14.7%	19.7%	11.4%	8.3%
Honors students	17.5%	14.7%	19.7%	5.7%	5.6%
Students in specific majors	15.9%	17.1%	18.0%	8.6%	16.7%
Learning community participants	13.4%	17.8%	23.0%	17.1%	8.3%
Other*	53.2%	41.1%	32.8%	25.7%	22.2%
None*	14.5%	30.2%	24.6%	51.4%	44.4%

Note. Percentages do not equal 100%. Respondents could make more than one selection.
*$p < .05$

Table 3.64

Type of Students Required to Take Seminar by Seminar Type (N = 772)

Students required to take seminar	EO (*n* = 316)	AUC (*n* = 134)	AVC (*n* = 138)	BSS (*n* = 45)	PRE (*n* = 12)	Hybrid (*n* = 125)
Provisionally admitted students*	20.3	19.4	15.2	40.0	16.7	20.8
Undeclared students	17.1	18.7	15.2	4.4	25.0	17.6
Student athletes	17.4	18.7	15.9	4.4	25.0	16.8
Honors students	15.2	19.4	18.1	4.4	25.0	17.6
Students in specific majors*	14.2	16.4	14.5	13.3	75.0	16.0
Learning community participants	16.5	17.2	13.0	2.2	33.3	14.4
Other	47.2	50.8	47.8	28.9	16.7	48.0
None*	21.5	12.7	27.5	35.6	0.0	18.4

Note. Percentages do not equal 100%. Respondents could make more than one selection. When *n* for seminar type <10, data were omitted from table.

*$p < .05$

Special Sections of Seminar

More than 20% of participating institutions reported that they offered special sections for honors students, and nearly 20% reported that they offered special sections for academically underprepared students and learning community participants. Public institutions and large institutions (those with more than 5,000 students) were more likely to offer special sections than private and small schools (Tables 3.65-3.69).

Table 3.65

Percentage of Special Sections Offered Across All Institutions (N = 821)

Student population for special section	Frequency	Percentage
Honors students	184	22.4
Academically underprepared students	163	19.9
Learning community participants	151	18.4
Students within a specific major	138	16.8
Undeclared students	72	8.8
Student athletes	69	8.4
Transfer students	53	6.5
Pre-professional students	45	5.5
International students	31	3.8
Students residing within a particular residence hall	30	3.7
Other	78	9.5
No special sections are offered	313	38.1

Note. Percentages do not equal 100%. Respondents could make more than one selection.

Table 3.66

Percentage of Special Sections Offered by Institutional Affiliation (N = 667)

Student population for special section	Private (n = 351)	Public (n = 316)
Honors students	23.7	23.1
Academically underprepared students**	13.1	25.6
Learning community participants**	10.8	27.5
Students within a specific major**	12.3	24.1
Undeclared students*	7.4	12.3
Student athletes**	4.6	12.7
Transfer students	8.0	6.3
Pre-professional students*	4.0	7.6
International students	3.7	3.8
Students residing within a particular residence hall	3.4	5.1
Other	8.6	11.4
No special sections are offered**	43.9	31.7

Note. Percentages do not equal 100%. Respondents could make more than one selection.

$^*p$ < .05. $^{**}p$ < .01.

Table 3.67

Percentage of Special Sections Offered by Institutional Type (*N* = 807)

Student population for special section	Two-year (*n* = 188)	Four-year (*n* = 619)
Honors students**	5.9	27.6
Academically underprepared students*	25.5	18.3
Learning community participants	14.9	19.6
Students within a specific major*	11.2	17.9
Undeclared students*	2.7	10.2
Student athletes	7.5	8.4
Transfer students**	2.1	7.8
Pre-professional students	2.7	6.3
International students	4.8	3.6
Students residing within a particular residence hall*	0.5	4.7
Other	10.6	9.4
No special sections are offered	41.0	37.2

Note. Percentages do not equal 100%. Respondents could make more than one selection.

*$p < .05$. **$p < .01$.

Table 3.68

Percentage of Special Sections Offered by Institutional Selectivity (N = 821)

Student population for special section	High (n = 117)	Other (n = 704)
Honors students	22.2	22.4
Academically underprepared students**	5.1	22.3
Learning community participants	14.5	19.0
Students within a specific major*	7.7	18.3
Undeclared students*	3.4	9.7
Student athletes	6.0	8.8
Transfer students	6.0	6.5
Pre-professional students	1.7	6.1
International students	4.3	3.7
Students residing within a particular residence hall**	8.6	2.8
Other	6.0	10.1
No special sections are offered**	50.4	36.1

Note. Percentages do not equal 100%. Respondents could make more than one selection.

*p < .05. **p < .01.

Table 3.69

Percentage of Special Sections Offered by Institutional Size (N = 821)

Student population for special section	5,000 or less (*n* = 560)	5,001-10,000 (*n* = 129)	10,001-15,000 (*n* = 61)	15,001-20,000 (*n* = 35)	More than 20,000 (*n* = 36)
Honors students*	19.3	24.8	26.2	31.4	47.2
Academically underprepared students*	15.9	26.4	29.5	31.4	30.6
Learning community participants*	10.7	24.0	42.6	48.6	47.2
Students within a specific major*	12.9	23.3	29.5	25.7	25.0
Undeclared students*	7.1	10.9	8.2	22.9	13.9
Student Athletes*	4.3	15.5	14.8	25.7	19.4
Transfer students*	5.7	6.2	4.9	11.4	16.7
Pre-professional students*	3.8	7.8	9.8	11.4	11.1
International students	3.2	3.9	6.6	2.9	8.3
Students residing within a particular residence hall*	2.0	5.4	9.8	8.6	8.3
Other	8.2	13.2	14.8	11.4	5.6
No special sections are offered*	43.9	33.3	13.1	14.3	30.6

Note. Percentages do not equal 100%. Respondents could make more than one selection.

*$p < .05$

Academic Credit

More than 90% of all participating institutions reported that their first-year seminar carried credit towards graduation, with highly selectively institutions more likely to offer credit than less selective institutions (97.3% vs. 91.4%). The largest proportion of institutions reported that they offered their seminar for one credit hour (42.5%) or three credit hours (32.7%). Less selective institutions were more likely to offer the seminar for one or three credit hours, whereas highly selective institutions were more likely to offer their seminar for four or more than five credit hours. More than half of extended orientation seminars (62.6%) carried one credit hour. The majority of schools also applied credit to a general education requirement (50.4%) or as an elective (40.3%). Private and highly selective institutions were more likely to apply credit toward a general education requirement than public and less selective institutions (Tables 3.70-3.87).

Table 3.70

Percentage of Seminars That Carry Credit Toward Graduation Across All Institutions (N = 805)

	Yes	No
Frequency	742	63
Percentage	92.2	7.8

Table 3.71

Percentage of Seminars That Carry Credit Toward Graduation by Institutional Affiliation (N = 652)

	Private (n = 343)	Public (n = 309)
Frequency	317	284
Percentage	92.4	91.9

Table 3.72

Percentage of Seminars That Carry Credit Toward Graduation by Institutional Type (N = 792)

	Two-year (n = 185)	Four-year (n = 607)
Frequency	165	565
Percentage	89.2	93.1

Table 3.73

Percentage of Seminars That Carry Credit Toward Graduation by Institutional Selectivity (N = 805)

	High (n = 111)	Other (n = 694)
Frequency	108	634
Percentage	97.3	91.4

$p < .05$

Table 3.74

Percentage of Seminars That Carry Credit Toward Graduation by Institutional Size (N = 805)

	5,000 or less (n = 550)	5,001 - 10,000 (n = 127)	10,001 - 15,000 (n = 59)	15,001 - 20,000 (n = 33)	More than 20,000 (n = 36)
Frequency	503	118	56	31	34
Percentage	91.5	92.9	94.9	93.9	94.4

Table 3.75
Percentage of Seminars That Carry Credit Toward Graduation by Seminar Type (*N* = 759)

	EO (*n* = 313)	AUC (*n* = 131)	AVC (*n* = 136)	BSS (*n* = 44)	PRE (*n* = 11)	Hybrid (*n* = 122)
Frequency	277	130	133	38	11	110
Percentage	88.5	99.2	97.8	86.4	100.0	90.2

Note. When *n* for seminar type <10, data were omitted from table.
p < .05

Table 3.76
Credit Hours Offered Across All Institutions (*N* = 737)

Number of credit hours	Frequency	Percentage
One	313	42.5
Two	93	12.6
Three	241	32.7
Four	66	9.0
Five	5	0.7
More than five	19	2.6

Table 3.77
Credit Hours Offered by Institutional Affiliation (*N* = 596)

Number of credit hours	Private (*n* = 315)	Public (*n* = 281)
One	45.4%	44.1%
Two*	8.3%	15.3%
Three*	26.4%	36.3%
Four**	16.2%	1.8%
Five	0.3%	1.1%
More than five	3.5%	1.4%

*p < .05. **p < .01.

Table 3.78
Credit Hours Offered by Institutional Type (N = 725)

Number of credit hours	Two-year (*n* = 165)	Four-year (*n* = 560)
One	45.5%	41.6%
Two	13.3%	11.8%
Three	37.6%	31.8%
Four*	0.6%	11.4%
Five	1.2%	0.5%
More than five	1.8%	2.9%

*$p < .01$

Table 3.79
Credit Hours Offered by Institutional Selectivity (N = 737)

Number of credit hours	High (*n* = 105)	Other (*n* = 632)
One*	26.7%	45.1%
Two	9.5%	13.1%
Three*	20.0%	34.8%
Four*	35.2%	4.6%
Five	1.0%	0.6%
More than five*	7.6%	1.7%

*$p < .01$

Table 3.80
Credit Hours Offered by Institutional Size (N = 737)

Number of credit hours	5,000 or less (*n* = 500)	5,001 - 10,000 (*n* = 117)	10,001 - 15,000 (*n* = 56)	15,001 - 20,000 (*n* = 30)	More than 20,000 (*n* = 34)
One	46.4%	37.6%	28.6%	36.7%	29.4%
Two	8.8 %	17.1%	26.8%	20.0%	23.5%
Three	30.0%	38.5%	37.5%	40.0%	38.2%
Four	11.8%	4.3%	3.6%	0.0%	0.0%
Five	0.2%	1.7%	3.6%	0.0%	0.0%
More than five	2.8%	0.9%	0.0%	3.3%	8.8%

$p < .05$

Table 3.81

Credit Hours Offered by Seminar Type (*N* = 696)

Number of credit hours	EO (*n* = 275)	AUC (*n* = 130)	AVC (*n* = 132)	BSS (*n* = 38)	PRE (*n* = 11)	Hybrid (*n* = 108)
One*	62.6%	29.2%	18.2%	29.0%	27.3%	43.5%
Two	15.6 %	10.0%	9.1%	13.2%	18.2%	12.0%
Three*	21.5%	43.1%	40.9%	50.0%	45.5%	29.6%
Four*	0.4%	10.8%	27.3%	0.0%	9.1%	10.2%
Five	0.0%	0.8%	1.5%	5.3%	0.0%	0.0%
More than five	0.0%	6.2%	3.0%	2.6%	0.0%	4.6%

Note. When *n* for seminar type <10, data were omitted from table.

*$p < .05$.

Table 3.82

Application of Credit Across All Institutions (*N* = 821)

Credit applied toward	Frequency	Percentage
General education	414	50.4
Elective	331	40.3
Major	76	9.3
Other	50	6.1

Note. Percentages do not equal 100%. Respondents could make more than one selection.

Table 3.83

Application of Credit by Institutional Affiliation (*N* = 667)

Credit applied toward	Private (*n* = 351)	Public (*n* = 316)
General education**	69.0%	32.3%
Elective**	23.7%	56.7%
Major*	6.8%	12.0%
Other	4.3%	7.0%

Note. Percentages do not equal 100%. Respondents could make more than one selection.

*$p < .05$. **$p < .01$.

Table 3.84
Application of Credit by Institutional Type (*N* = 807)

Credit applied toward	Two-year (*n* = 188)	Four-year (*n* = 619)
General education**	29.3%	57.0%
Elective**	55.9%	35.5%
Major	9.0%	9.2%
Other*	10.1%	4.9%

Note. Percentages do not equal 100%. Respondents could make more than one selection.
*p < .05. **p < .01.

Table 3.85
Application of Credit by Institutional Selectivity (*N* = 821)

Credit applied toward	High (*n* = 117)	Other (*n* = 704)
General education*	66.7%	47.7%
Elective	35.0%	41.2%
Major	13.7%	8.5%
Other	4.3%	6.4%

Note. Percentages do not equal 100%. Respondents could make more than one selection.
*p < .01

Table 3.86
Application of Credit by Institutional Size (*N* = 821)

Credit applied toward	5,000 or less (*n* = 560)	5,001 - 10,000 (*n* = 129)	10,001 - 15,000 (*n* = 61)	15,001 - 20,000 (*n* = 35)	More than 20,000 (*n* = 36)
General education*	56.8%	39.5%	34.4%	20.0%	47.2%
Elective*	30.7%	57.4%	57.4%	71.4%	69.4%
Major*	7.5%	16.3%	8.2%	8.6%	13.9%
Other	5.0%	7.8%	11.5%	11.4%	2.8%

Note. Percentages do not equal 100%. Respondents could make more than one selection.
*p < .05

Table 3.87

Application of Credit by Seminar Type (N = 772)

Credit applied toward	EO (*n* = 316)	AUC (*n* = 134)	AVC (*n* = 138)	BSS (*n* = 45)	PRE (*n* = 12)	Hybrid (*n* = 125)
General education*	33.9%	76.9%	75.4%	8.9%	58.3%	47.2%
As an elective*	49.7%	22.4%	33.3%	66.7%	8.33%	44.0%
Major*	7.3%	6.7%	14.5%	11.1%	41.7%	8.8%
Other	7.6%	3.0%	5.1%	8.9%	0.0%	5.6%

Note. Percentages do not equal 100%. Respondents could make more than one selection. When *n* for seminar type <10, data were omitted from table.

*$p < .05$

Grading

Most institutions reported that their seminar was letter graded (82.0%). This was true at public and private schools (81.5% vs. 80.8%, respectively), two- and four-year institutions (84.9% vs. 81.4%, respectively), and regardless of selectivity (82.5% high selectivity vs. 82% all others) (Tables 3.88-3.93).

Table 3.88

Method of Grading Across All Institutions (N = 810)

Grade type	Frequency	Percentage
Letter grade	664	82.0
Pass/fail	126	15.6
No grade	20	2.5

Table 3.89

Method of Grading by Institutional Affiliation (N = 657)

Grade type	Private (*n* = 349)	Public (*n* = 308)
Letter grade	80.8%	81.5%
Pass/fail	17.8%	14.9%
No grade	1.4%	3.6%

Table 3.90

Method of Grading by Institutional Type (*N* = 797)

Grade type	Two-year (*n* = 185)	Four-year (*n* = 612)
Letter grade	84.9%	81.4%
Pass/fail	11.4%	16.5%
No grade	3.8%	2.1%

Table 3.91

Method of Grading by Institutional Selectivity (*N* = 810)

Grade type	High (*n* = 114)	Other (*n* = 696)
Letter grade	82.5%	82.0%
Pass/fail	17.5%	15.2%
No grade	0.0%	2.9%

Table 3.92

Method of Grading by Institutional Size (*N* = 810)

Grade type	5,000 or less (*n* = 557)	5,001 - 10,000 (*n* = 125)	10,001 - 15,000 (*n* = 59)	15,001 - 20,000 (*n* = 33)	More than 20,000 (*n* = 36)
Letter grade	81.9%	84.0%	88.1%	75.8%	72.2%
Pass/fail	16.0%	12.8%	6.8%	21.2%	27.8%
No grade	2.2%	3.2%	5.1%	3.0%	0.0%

Table 3.93

Method of Grading by Seminar Type (*N* = 764)

Grade type	EO (*n* = 310)	AUC (*n* = 134)	AVC (*n* = 138)	BSS (*n* = 44)	PRE (*n* = 12)	Hybrid (*n* = 124)
Letter grade	75.5%	89.6%	91.3%	79.6%	100.0%	82.3%
Pass/fail	20.3%	9.7%	8.0%	20.5%	0.0%	14.5%
No grade	4.2%	0.8%	0.7%	0.0%	0.0%	3.2%

Note. When *n* for seminar type <10, data were omitted from table.

$p < .05$

Seminar Contact Hours

The vast majority of participating institutions reported that they offered seminars with one to three total contact hours per week. Highly selective schools were more likely to offer seminars with more contact hours (three or four contact hours per week), while less selective schools were more likely to offer seminars with one or two contact hours per week (Tables 3.94-3.99).

Table 3.94
Contact Hours per Week Across All Institutions (N = 804)

Number of contact hours	Frequency	Percentage
One	222	27.6
Two	186	23.1
Three	311	38.7
Four	50	6.2
Five	7	0.9
More than five	28	3.5

Table 3.95
Contact Hours per Week by Institutional Affiliation (N = 652)

Number of contact hours	Private (*n* = 344)	Public (*n* = 308)
One	30.2%	30.2%
Two	20.1%	26.0%
Three	36.6%	36.7%
Four*	9.0%	2.9%
Five	0.6%	1.0%
More than five	3.5%	3.3%

*$p < .01$

Table 3.96

Contact Hours per Week by Institutional Type (N = 791)

Number of contact hours	Two-year (*n* = 184)	Four-year (*n* = 607)
One	26.6%	27.8%
Two	22.3%	22.9%
Three	38.0%	39.4%
Four	4.4%	6.9%
Five	2.2%	0.5%
More than five*	6.5%	2.5%

*$p < .05$

Table 3.97

Contact Hours per Week by Institutional Selectivity (N = 804)

Number of contact hours	High (*n* = 112)	Other (*n* = 692)
One**	15.2%	29.6%
Two**	13.4%	24.7%
Three*	50.0%	36.9%
Four**	15.2%	4.8%
Five	0.9%	0.9%
More than five	5.4%	3.2%

*$p < .05$. **$p < .01$.

Table 3.98

Contact Hours per Week by Institutional Size (N = 804)

Number of contact hours	5,000 or less (*n* = 551)	5,001 - 10,000 (*n* = 125)	10,001 - 15,000 (*n* = 59)	15,001 - 20,000 (*n* = 33)	More than 20,000 (*n* = 36)
One	29.4%	22.4%	25.4%	21.2%	27.8%
Two	20.9%	28.0 %	28.8%	33.3%	22.2%
Three	38.1%	43.2%	35.6%	39.4%	36.1%
Four	7.6%	3.2%	5.1%	3.0%	0.0%
Five	0.7%	1.6%	1.7%	0.0%	0.0%
More than five	3.3%	1.6%	3.4%	3.0%	13.9%

Table 3.99

Contact Hours per Week by Seminar Type (N = 758)

Number of contact hours	EO (*n* = 307)	AUC (*n* = 134)	AVC (*n* = 137)	BSS (*n* = 44)	PRE (*n* = 12)	Hybrid (*n* = 122)
One*	43.7%	17.2%	9.5%	13.6%	16.7%	27.1%
Two	27.7%	20.9%	11.7%	20.5%	16.7%	24.6%
Three*	23.5%	50.0%	59.1%	54.6%	58.3%	37.7%
Four	1.3%	8.2%	15.3%	2.3%	8.3%	7.4%
Five	0.3%	0.8%	1.5%	4.6%	0.0%	0.0%
More than five	3.6%	3.0%	2.9%	4.6%	0.0%	3.3%

Note. When *n* for seminar type <10, data were omitted from table.

*$p < .05$

Course Topics

The survey asked respondents to list the three most important topics in their first-year seminars. The most frequently selected topics were study skills (40.8%), critical thinking (40.6%), campus resources (38.1%), academic planning/advising (36.7%), and time management (28.6%).

Not surprisingly, the most important course topics varied by institutional affiliation, selectivity, and seminar type. Study skills, campus resources, and time management were selected as important topics at public institutions (50.6%, 47.2%, and 34.5%, respectively) more often than at private ones (27.6%, 30.2%, and 21.1%, respectively). Further, private institutions selected critical thinking skills (45.6% private institutions vs. 32.9% public institutions), writing skills (30.8% vs. 12.0%), relationship issues (17.4% vs. 10.8%), and diversity issues (13.4% vs. 6.0%) significantly more often than public institutions.

Four-year institutions most often reported that critical thinking (46.0%) was the most important topic in their first-year seminar. However, a much smaller proportion (25.0%) of two-year institutions specified critical thinking as the primary course topic in their seminar. Almost two thirds of the participating two-year institutions identified study skills as the most common course topic, but approximately one third of the four-year institutions listed it as one of the primary topics. (See Table 3.102.) This differential may be a reflection of the fact that a greater number of two-year institutions are nonselective and provide remedial education in contrast to four-year institutions (Cohen & Brawer, 1996).

Highly selective institutions selected critical thinking (67.5% vs. 36.1%), writing skills (45.3% vs. 17.8%), and specific disciplinary topic (35.0% vs. 12.9%) more often than less selective ones. Critical thinking was selected most frequently by institutions offering primarily academic seminars—both those with uniform content (63.4%) and those with variable content (74.6%), as well as by schools offering primarily pre-professional (50.0%) and hybrid seminars (44.0%) (Tables 3.100-3.105).

Table 3.100
Most Important Course Topics Across All Institutions (*N* = 821)

Course topic	Frequency	Percentage
Study skills	335	40.8
Critical thinking	333	40.6
Campus resources	313	38.1
Academic planning/advising	301	36.7
Time management	235	28.6
Writing skills	178	21.7
Career exploration/preparation	145	17.7
Specific disciplinary topic	132	16.1
College policies & procedures	117	14.3
Relationship issues	114	13.9
Diversity issues	79	9.6
Other	110	13.4

Note. Percentages do not equal 100%. Respondents could make more than one selection.

Table 3.101
Most Important Course Topics by Institutional Affiliation (*N* = 667)

Course topic	Private (*n* = 351)	Public (*n* = 316)
Study skills**	27.6%	50.6%
Critical thinking**	45.6%	32.9%
Campus resources**	30.2%	47.2%
Academic planning/advising	34.2%	39.6%
Time management**	21.1%	34.5%
Writing skills**	30.8%	12.0%
Career exploration/preparation**	12.8%	21.2%
Specific disciplinary topic	18.2%	14.6%
College policies & procedures*	11.7%	18.0%
Relationship issues*	17.4%	10.8%
Diversity issues**	13.4%	6.0%
Other**	18.5%	8.9%

Note. Percentages do not equal 100%. Respondents could make more than one selection.
*$p < .05$. **$p < .01$.

Table 3.102

Most Important Course Topics by Institutional Type (N = 807)

Course topic	Two-year (*n* = 188)	Four-year (*n* = 619)
Study skills**	64.9%	33.3%
Critical thinking**	25.0%	46.0%
Campus resources**	52.7%	33.6%
Academic planning/advising	39.9%	36.0%
Time management**	41.0%	24.2%
Writing skills**	6.4%	26.7%
Career exploration/preparation**	30.9%	13.4%
Specific disciplinary topic**	4.3%	19.6%
College policies & procedures	16.0%	13.1%
Relationship issues	13.8%	13.6%
Diversity issues*	2.7%	11.5%
Other**	4.8%	15.8%

Note. Percentages do not equal 100%. Respondents could make more than one selection.
**p* < .05. ***p* < .01.

Table 3.103

Most Important Course Topics by Institutional Selectivity (N = 821)

Course topic	High (*n* = 117)	Other (*n* = 704)
Study skills**	12.8%	45.5%
Critical thinking**	67.5%	36.1%
Campus resources**	17.1%	41.6%
Academic planning/advising**	23.1%	38.9%
Time management**	7.7%	32.1%
Writing skills**	45.3%	17.8%
Career exploration/preparation**	7.7%	19.3%
Specific disciplinary topic**	35.0%	12.9%
College policies & procedures**	5.1%	15.8%
Relationship issues**	4.3%	15.5%
Diversity issues	9.4%	9.7%
Other*	20.5%	12.2%

Note. Percentages do not equal 100%. Respondents could make more than one selection.
**p* < .05. ***p* < .01.

Table 3.104

Most Important Course Topics by Institutional Size (*N* = 821)

Course topic	5,000 or less (*n* = 560)	5,001 - 10,000 (*n* = 129)	10,001 - 15,000 (*n* = 61)	15,001 - 20,000 (*n* = 35)	More than 20,000 (*n* = 36)
Study skills*	37.9%	45.7%	47.5%	62.9%	36.1%
Critical thinking	41.8%	41.9%	34.4%	31.4%	36.1%
Campus resources*	35.2%	39.5%	55.7%	51.4%	36.1%
Academic planning/ advising	36.1%	37.2%	37.8%	42.9%	36.1%
Time management	27.0%	33.3%	36.1%	37.1%	16.7%
Writing skills	24.5%	17.8%	13.1%	11.4%	16.7%
Career exploration/ preparation	16.1%	23.3%	18.0%	25.7%	13.9%
Specific disciplinary topic*	14.3%	22.5%	6.6%	8.6%	44.4%
College policies & procedures	14.1%	16.3%	11.5%	14.3%	13.9%
Relationship issues*	17.1%	7.0%	8.2%	8.6%	2.8%
Diversity issues	10.5%	7.0%	9.8%	5.7%	8.3%
Other*	15.4%	10.1%	3.3%	8.6%	16.7%

Note. Percentages do not equal 100%. Respondents could make more than one selection.

*p < .05

Table 3.105
Most Important Course Topics by Seminar Type (*N* = 772)

Course topic	EO (*n* = 316)	AUC (*n* = 134)	AVC (*n* = 138)	BSS (*n* = 45)	PRE (*n* = 12)	Hybrid (*n* = 125)
Study skills*	55.1%	27.6%	18.1%	75.6%	25.0%	36.0%
Critical thinking*	15.8%	63.4%	74.6%	31.1%	50.0%	44.0%
Campus resources*	57.9%	26.1%	10.9%	35.6%	25.0%	36.8%
Academic planning/ advising*	48.1%	26.1%	19.6%	40.0%	41.7%	32.8%
Time management*	40.5%	16.4%	7.3%	57.8%	16.7%	24.8%
Writing skills*	5.1%	37.3%	56.5%	8.9%	8.3%	16.0%
Career exploration/ preparation*	21.2%	16.4%	3.6%	33.3%	50.0%	18.4%
Specific disciplinary topic*	1.9%	12.7%	50.7%	4.4%	41.7%	17.6%
College policies & procedures*	22.5%	12.7%	2.9%	8.9%	25.0%	8.8%
Relationship issues*	21.2%	12.7%	2.9%	8.9%	8.3%	9.6%
Diversity issues*	5.4%	22.4%	6.5%	2.2%	8.3%	8.8%
Other*	5.7%	23.9%	18.1%	2.2%	8.3%	21.6%

Note. Percentages do not equal 100%. Respondents could make more than one selection.
When *n* for seminar type <10, data were omitted from table.
*$p < .05$

Administration

Departmental Home

Most participating institutions indicated that the division of academic affairs was the administrative home of their seminar (50.8%), with only 10.5% stating that the seminar was administered by first-year program offices. Public institutions were more likely to administer seminars through student affairs and academic departments than private institutions. Academic affairs (38.3%), an academic department (26.8%), and student affairs (23.5%) were more likely to be the campus unit that administered the course at two-year campuses. At four-year institutions, the seminar was much more likely to be administered through academic affairs (55.0%) (Tables 3.106-3.111).

Table 3.106
Administrative Home of First-Year Seminar Across All Institutions (N = 791)

Administrative home	Frequency	Percentage
Academic affairs	402	50.8
Academic department	107	13.5
Student affairs	102	12.9
First-year program office	83	10.5
Other	97	12.3

Table 3.107
Administrative Home of First-Year Seminar by Institutional Affiliation (N = 644)

Administrative home	Private (n = 342)	Public (n = 302)
Academic affairs*	57.0%	42.1%
Academic department*	8.2%	16.9%
Student affairs*	9.4%	16.9%
First-year program office	14.0%	9.3%
Other	11.4%	14.9%

*$p < .01$

Table 3.108
Administrative Home of First-Year Seminar by Institutional Type (N = 778)

Administrative home	Two-year (n = 183)	Four-year (n = 595)
Academic affairs*	38.3%	55.0%
Academic department*	26.8%	9.6%
Student affairs*	23.5%	9.4%
First-year program office*	2.2%	12.9%
Other	9.3%	13.1%

*$p < .01$

Table 3.109

Administrative Home of First-Year Seminar by Institutional Selectivity (*N* = 791)

Administrative home	High (*n* = 109)	Other (*n* = 682)
Academic affairs	55.1%	50.2%
Academic department	9.2%	14.2%
Student affairs*	4.6%	14.2%
First-year program office*	16.5%	9.5%
Other	14.7%	11.9%

*p < .05

Table 3.110

Administrative Home of First-Year Seminar by Institutional Size (*N* = 791)

Administrative home	5,000 or less (*n* = 545)	5,001 - 10,000 (*n* = 122)	10,001 - 15,000 (*n* = 58)	15,001 - 20,000 (*n* = 32)	More than 20,000 (*n* = 34)
Academic affairs*	55.1%	42.6%	43.1%	31.3%	44.1%
Academic department	13.8%	14.8%	13.8%	9.4%	8.8%
Student affairs*	10.8%	17.2%	17.2%	28.1%	8.8%
First-year program office	10.5%	9.8%	8.6%	15.6%	11.8%
Other*	9.9%	15.6%	17.2%	15.6%	26.5%

*p < .05

Table 3.111

Administrative Home of First-Year Seminar by Seminar Type (*N* = 748)

Administrative home	EO (*n* = 306)	AUC (*n* = 131)	AVC (*n* = 133)	BSS (*n* = 43)	PRE (*n* = 12)	Hybrid (*n* = 121)
Academic affairs*	42.8%	61.8%	63.2%	39.5%	41.7%	51.2%
Academic department*	12.1%	11.5%	9.8%	39.5%	33.3%	12.4%
Student affairs*	21.2%	6.9%	1.5%	16.3%	0.0%	9.1%
First-year program office	11.4%	10.7%	11.3%	0.0%	8.3%	9.9%
Other	12.4%	9.2%	14.3%	4.7%	16.7%	17.4%

Note. When *n* for seminar type <10, data were omitted from table.

*p < .05

Course Leadership

Almost 80% of respondents indicated that the seminar had a dean/director/coordinator, and more than 60% reported that this position was less than full-time. Across all institutions, almost 50% of the deans/directors/coordinators who held other positions were members of the faculty. On two-year campuses, the other position held by course directors was typically a student affairs position (30.5%) or faculty (28.8%). At four-year institutions, the other role was more likely to be faculty (52.8%) (Tables 3.112-3.129).

Table 3.112
Seminar Has Dean/Director/Coordinator Across All Institutions (N = 795)

	Yes	No
Frequency	634	161
Percentage	79.8	20.3

Table 3.113
Seminar Has Dean/Director/Coordinator by Institutional Affiliation (N = 649)

	Private (*n* = 342)	Public (*n* = 307)
Frequency	299	230
Percentage	87.4	74.9

p < .05

Table 3.114
Seminar Has Dean/Director/Coordinator by Institutional Type (N = 781)

	Two-year (*n* = 183)	Four-year (*n* = 598)
Frequency	123	503
Percentage	67.2	84.1

p < .05

Table 3.115
Seminar Has Dean/Director/Coordinator by Institutional Selectivity (N = 795)

	High (*n* =112)	Other (*n* = 683)
Frequency	89	545
Percentage	79.5	79.8

Table 3.116

Seminar Has Dean/Director/Coordinator by Institutional Size (N = 795)

	5,000 or less (n = 544)	5,001 - 10,000 (n = 123)	10,001 - 15,000 (n = 59)	15,001 - 20,000 (n = 33)	More than 20,000 (n = 36)
Frequency	437	94	46	26	31
Percentage	80.3	76.4	78.0	78.8	86.1

Table 3.117

Seminar Has Dean/Director/Coordinator by Seminar Type (N = 751)

	EO (n = 312)	AUC (n = 127)	AVC (n = 136)	BSS (n = 43)	PRE (n = 11)	Hybrid (n = 120)
Frequency	250	109	115	22	3	95
Percentage	80.1	85.8	84.6	51.2	27.3	79.2

Note. When n for seminar type <10, data were omitted from table.

$p < .05$

Table 3.118

Status of Dean/Director/Coordinator Across All Institutions (N = 628)

Status	Frequency	Percentage
Full time	238	37.9
Less than full time	390	62.1

Table 3.119

Status of Dean/Director/Coordinator by Institutional Affiliation (N = 525)

Status	Private (n = 295)	Public (n = 230)
Full time	28.8%	47.8%
Less than full time	71.2%	52.2%

$p < .05$

Table 3.120

Status of Dean/Director/Coordinator by Institutional Type (N = 620)

Status	Two-year (n = 121)	Four-year (n = 499)
Full time	48.8%	35.5%
Less than full time	51.2%	64.5%

$p < .05$

Table 3.121
Status of Dean/Director/Coordinator by Institutional Selectivity (N = 628)

Status	High (*n* = 87)	Other (*n* = 541)
Full time	44.8%	36.8%
Less than full time	55.2%	63.2%

Table 3.122
Status of Dean/Director/Coordinator by Institutional Size (N = 628)

Status	5,000 or less (*n* = 433)	5,001 - 10,000 (*n* = 93)	10,001 - 15,000 (*n* = 46)	15,001 - 20,000 (*n* = 25)	More than 20,000 (*n* = 31)
Full time	30.5%	52.7%	54.3%	48.0%	64.5%
Less than full time	69.5%	47.3%	45.7%	52.0%	35.5%

$p < .05$

Table 3.123
Status of Dean/Director/Coordinator by Seminar Type (N = 590)

Status	EO (*n* = 249)	AUC (*n* = 109)	AVC (*n* = 113)	BSS (*n* = 22)	Hybrid (*n* = 92)
Full time	43.4%	33.9%	32.7%	50.0%	33.7%
Less than full time	56.6%	66.1%	67.3%	50.0%	66.3%

Note. When *n* for seminar type <10, data were omitted from table.

Table 3.124
Other Role of Dean/Director/Coordinator Across All Institutions (N = 374)

Other role	Frequency	Percentage
Faculty member	182	48.7
Academic affairs administrator	81	21.7
Student affairs administrator	59	15.8
Other	52	13.9

Table 3.125
Other Role of Dean/Director/Coordinator by Institutional Affiliation (*N* = 317)

Other role	Private (*n* = 203)	Public (*n* = 114)
Faculty member**	56.2%	33.3%
Academic affairs administrator	21.2%	22.8%
Student affairs administrator	12.8%	21.1%
Other**	9.9%	22.8%

**p < .01

Table 3.126
Other Role of Dean/Director/Coordinator by Institutional Type (*N* = 368)

Other role	Two-year (*n* = 59)	Four-year (*n* = 309)
Faculty member**	28.8%	52.8%
Academic affairs administrator	20.3%	22.0%
Student affairs administrator**	30.5%	12.3%
Other	20.3%	12.9%

**p < .01

Table 3.127
Other Role of Dean/Director/Coordinator by Institutional Selectivity (*N* = 374)

Other role	High (*n* = 46)	Other (*n* = 328)
Faculty member	63.0%	46.7%
Academic affairs administrator	19.6%	22.0%
Student affairs administrator	8.8%	16.8%
Other	8.7%	14.6%

Table 3.128

Other Role of Dean/Director/Coordinator by Institutional Size (N = 374)

	5,000 or less (*n* = 288)	5,001 - 10,000 (*n* = 42)	10,001 - 15,000 (*n* = 20)	15,001 - 20,000 (*n* = 13)	More than 20,000 (*n* = 11)
Faculty member	52.1%	45.2%	35.0%	15.4%	36.4%
Academic affairs administrator	21.5%	21.4%	25.0%	23.1%	18.2%
Student affairs administrator	13.2%	21.4%	15.0%	38.5%	36.4%
Other	13.2%	11.9%	25.0%	23.1%	9.1%

Table 3.129

Other Role of Dean/Director/Coordinator by Seminar Type (N = 349)

Other role	EO (*n* = 136)	AUC (*n* = 69)	AVC (*n* = 73)	BSS (*n* = 11)	Hybrid (*n* = 58)
Faculty member	27.2%	69.6%	63.0%	27.3%	55.2%
Academic affairs administrated	26.5%	20.3%	24.7%	45.5%	12.1%
Student affairs administrated	29.4%	4.4%	2.7%	9.1%	12.1%
Other	16.9%	5.8%	9.6%	18.2%	20.7%

Note. When *n* for seminar type <10, data were omitted from table.

p < .05

Innovative or Successful Course Components

In each survey administration since 2000, we have asked respondents to share some of their innovative or successful course components. Because this is an open-ended question, we are unable to determine the prevalence of any of these approaches. However, 540 institutions offered details regarding some of their innovative or successful course components. The methods mentioned tended to fall within the following areas: (a) course structure, (b) the use of technology, (c) activities/assignments, and (d) encouraging faculty/staff/student connections. Examples of innovative course components follow.

Course Structure

- Integrating the seminar into a learning community (Arkansas State University, Rollins College)
- Providing a weekly common period to schedule activities. Avila University used four Fridays to address career exploration and planning.
- Linking the course with a residence hall/floor (e.g., At Trinity College, students live together and take the course together.)

- Offering a version of the course before the beginning of the academic year. The seminar at Mohawk Valley Community College met one week prior to the start of classes in August. Highland Community College offered a one-week summer session for "academically talented students" that concentrated on critical thinking.
- Team-building session offered prior to start of classes (Graceland University) or held the first weekend of classes (William Penn University)
- Having a common schedule for the seminar. Lyme Academy College of Fine Arts offered all sections of the seminar at the same time and day so students would not forget. Instructors also provided food. Both elements led to an increase in attendance.
- Offering a yearlong seminar with the same instructor (Delaware State University). Some institutions did not offer yearlong courses, but they encouraged continued connections by having instructors "serve as coaches…throughout the first year and often into later years" (Rochester Institute of Technology).

Technology

- Offering an online virtual library tour (University of South Alabama)
- Using clickers in large classes (University of Missouri at Kansas City). These technological devices were bought by or provided to every student in a class. At points during the lesson, the instructor posed questions for students to answer. The clickers immediately provided frequencies for each of the multiple-choice answers.
- Having students create e-portfolios (University of Maine, Fort Kent College)
- Including online discussions after in-class meetings (Raritan Valley Community College)
- Requiring time in the computer lab. At Youngstown State University, students spent "one hour for 10 to 12 weeks each term in a computer-assisted instruction lab to increase their reading rate and comprehension."

Activities/Assignments

- Offering field trips. At Oglethorpe University, students visited Atlanta attractions (e.g., museums, plays, and/or historic sites). Students at Elms College took a field trip to the United Nations and New York City.
- Providing outdoor adventure opportunities (Northland College). At the University of Great Falls, "there are several opportunities for students to get out and see the state of Montana through rafting trips on the Missouri River, horseback riding on the Rocky Mountain Front, skiing together in the Little Belt Mountains… and an alternative spring break program to a major west coast city to serve others." Some institutions mentioned offering a Saturday ropes course with students and faculty (University of Portland).
- Offering common reading in the summer or during the regular term (Henderson State University, Bristol Community College, Illinois College, Drury University). Common readings may extend beyond a single text. At William Jewell College, there were several common texts including *On Liberty* by John Stuart Mill, *Consilience* by E.O. Wilson, and *Confessions* by St. Augustine. Other institutions created campus-specific textbooks (University of Kansas, Kennesaw State University, Sullivan County Community College).
- Engaging in service activities (Cal Polytechnic State University). At North Hennepin Community College, the class planted a garden (Growing College Success) and donated the produce to a local mosque and food bank.

- Integrating career and major exploration experiences (California State University, East Bay). Finlandia University offered an "Eat and Meet" where students were grouped by major and served lunch for one class session.
- Encouraging self-reflection. Students wrote an "I have a dream" speech about their own lives (Indiana Wesleyan University) or their own mission statements (Bennett College).
- Using scavenger hunts. Institutions used this approach to familiarize the students with key offices and resources (Central Bible College).
- Introducing the students to the library (North Central State College, Middlesex County College). This might include a library tour (Appalachian Bible College) or a librarian as one of the instructors (Washington State University). At Coastal Carolina University, a library instruction module introduced first-year students to doing "basic college-level research."

Faculty/Staff/Student Connections

- Organizing meetings with advisors out of class. Cloud County Community College required students to meet with their advisors in the first few weeks of the term.
- Organizing faculty interaction out of class. At La Sierra University, faculty kept in contact with a cohort of students by meeting at least once every three weeks with each student. UC Berkeley has a "Food for Thought" option, where faculty and students eat together before or after the seminar in the dining commons.
- Advisors teaching their advisees (Valdosta State University, Rollins College, Mercer College)
- Using peer leaders in the seminars (Austin College). At the University of La Verne, the peer assistants came from the "Landis Leadership" program, which recognized the top 1% of students and awarded a "scholarship ($6,000) for their work."

Conclusion

The snapshot of the seminar that emerged from the survey findings shows great variety depending on the type of seminar and the affiliation, size, and selectivity of an institution. Course topics and approaches depended greatly on the type of institution offering the seminar. Nevertheless, many consistencies were also evident. Seminars tended to be relatively small, offered credit that counts towards graduation, and were either academic (variable or uniform content) or an extended orientation. Many institutions required the seminar for all or at least some of their students, from honors students to students who are academically underprepared. Since the 2003 survey administration, we have seen an increase in the number of seminars that are embedded in learning communities, offer some of or the entire course online, and have service-learning components.

Notes

[1]The actual question was: Do any sections include a service-learning component (i.e., non-remunerative service as a part of a course)?

References

Cohen, A. M., & Brawer, F. B. (1996). *The American community college* (3rd ed.). San Francisco: Jossey-Bass.

Chapter 4

Seminar Instruction and Training

Barbara F. Tobolowsky and Angela Griffin

This chapter focuses on seminar instruction. It provides the details regarding who is responsible for seminar instruction, workload and compensation, and instructor training. All data are presented by institution type, affiliation, selectivity, size, and type of seminar.

Teaching Responsibility

Ninety percent of responding institutions used faculty to teach their first-year seminars. Student affairs professionals and other campus professionals (e.g., librarians and academic administrators) were also used at a number of campuses (45.2% and 26.8%, respectively). Private institutions were more likely than public institutions to use faculty (93.2% vs. 87.7%), while public institutions were more likely to use student affairs professionals (54.1% vs. 40.5%) and graduate students (8.2% vs. 3.1%). A large number of both highly selective and less selective institutions reported using faculty to teach their seminars. However, less selective ones reported using student affairs (47.9% vs. 29.1%) and other campus professionals (28.7% vs. 15.4%) more often than highly selective ones (Tables 4.1-4.6).

Table 4.1

Teaching Responsibility Across All Institutions (*N* = 821)

Instructor for seminar	Frequency	Percentage
Faculty	739	90.0
Student affairs professionals	371	45.2
Other campus professionals	220	26.8
Graduate students	43	5.2
Undergraduate students	63	7.7

Note. Percentages do not equal 100%. Respondents could make more than one selection.

Table 4.2
Teaching Responsibility by Institutional Affiliation (N = 667)

Instructor for seminar	Private (*n* = 351)	Public (*n* = 316)
Faculty*	93.2%	87.7%
Student affairs professionals**	40.5%	54.1%
Other campus professionals	26.8%	28.5%
Graduate students**	3.1%	8.2%
Undergraduate students	10.3%	6.0%

Note. Percentages do not equal 100%. Respondents could make more than one selection.
*$p < .05$. **$p < .01$.

Table 4.3
Teaching Responsibility by Institutional Type (N = 807)

Instructor for seminar	Two-year (*n* = 188)	Four-year (*n* = 619)
Faculty**	84.6%	91.6%
Student affairs professionals	45.2%	45.2%
Other campus professionals	22.3%	28.0%
Graduate students**	0.5%	6.6%
Undergraduate students**	0.5%	9.9%

Note. Percentages do not equal 100%. Respondents could make more than one selection.
**$p < .01$

Table 4.4
Teaching Responsibility by Institutional Selectivity (N = 821)

Instructor for seminar	High (*n* = 117)	Other (*n* = 704)
Faculty	93.2%	89.5%
Student affairs professionals**	29.1%	47.9%
Other campus professionals**	15.4%	28.7%
Graduate students	3.4%	5.5%
Undergraduate students	6.0%	8.0%

Note. Percentages do not equal 100%. Respondents could make more than one selection.
**$p < .01$

Table 4.5

Teaching Responsibility by Institutional Size (N = 821)

Instructor for seminar	5,000 or less (n = 560)	5,001 - 10,000 (n = 129)	10,001 - 15,000 (n = 61)	15,001 - 20,000 (n = 35)	More than 20,000 (n = 36)
Faculty*	91.1%	89.2%	90.2%	74.3%	91.7%
Student affairs professionals*	41.6%	51.9%	59.0%	60.0%	38.9%
Other campus professionals	27.3%	22.5%	27.9%	42.9%	16.7%
Graduate students*	2.5%	6.2%	13.1%	20.0%	16.7%
Undergraduate students*	7.0%	7.8%	4.9%	22.9%	8.3%

Note. Percentages do not equal 100%. Respondents could make more than one selection.

*$p < .05$

Table 4.6

Teaching Responsibility by Seminar Type (N = 772)

Instructor for seminar	EO (n = 316)	AUC (n = 134)	AVC (n = 138)	BSS (n = 45)	PRE (n = 12)	Hybrid (n = 125)
Faculty*	84.8%	95.5%	97.8%	86.7%	100.0%	88.8%
Student affairs professionals*	63.3%	38.8%	23.9%	26.7%	16.7%	41.6%
Other campus professionals*	36.7%	20.2 %	12.3%	13.3%	16.7%	32.8%
Graduate students	7.0%	3.7%	2.9%	0.0%	16.7%	6.4%
Undergraduate students*	11.1%	2.2%	6.5%	0.0%	16.7%	8.8%

Note. Percentages do not equal 100%. Respondents could make more than one selection. When n for seminar type < 10, data were omitted from the table.

*$p < .05$

Team Teaching

While almost half (43.7%) of responding institutions had some sections that were team-taught, very few institutions employed team-teaching in all their seminar sections (only 11.4%) (Tables 4.7-4.18). Of those respondents who used team teaching, 259 provided some details regarding their team-teaching configurations. Typically, responding institutions with team-taught sections used teams composed of faculty with professional staff, faculty with faculty, faculty with undergraduate student(s), staff with staff, staff with undergraduate student(s), or faculty with graduate student(s). However, a number of other institutions mentioned more unique team configurations. For instance, some teams were large. At

Baker College, teams were composed of faculty, academic advisors, librarians, and the Learning Center director. At Iowa Lakes Community College, faculty, counselors, career resource, and success center staff team-taught the course. Some institutions described unique course designs, which require different teaching configurations. For example, at Texas State Technical College in Harlingen, the seminar included a lecture taught by student success advisors and a lab taught by computer information systems faculty. At Master's College, a different teacher led the seminar class each week.

Some respondents talked about campus leaders teaching the seminar. For example, at Blue Mountain College, the college president taught a section independently, and the vice president of academic affairs team-taught another section with the director of the Center for the Advancement of Learning. Two vice presidents taught a section at American International College. At Carlow University, two academic deans and three science faculty team-taught the first-year seminar.

A number of respondents relied on students for seminar instruction. At New Mexico Highlands University, "teams of five graduate students with one primary instructor" taught the course. From this description, it is not clear the rank or role of that primary instructor, but it is a unique configuration. Undergraduate peer counselors team-taught a section at the University of Texas at Arlington. Clearly, it seems that if you can think of a teaching configuration, it is quite likely that it has been done at some college or university.

Table 4.7

Percentage of Institutions Reporting Team-Taught Sections Across All Institutions ($N = 789$)

	Frequency	Percentage
Yes	345	43.7
No	444	56.3

Table 4.8

Percentage of Institutions Reporting Team-Taught Sections by Institutional Affiliation ($N = 644$)

	Private ($n = 342$)	Public ($n = 302$)
Yes	44.7%	44.7%
No	55.3%	55.3%

Table 4.9

Percentage of Institutions Reporting Team-Taught Sections by Institutional Type ($N = 776$)

	Two-year ($n = 180$)	Four-year ($n = 596$)
Yes	33.9%	46.3%
No	66.1%	53.7%

$p < .01$

Table 4.10

Percentage of Institutions Reporting Team-Taught Sections by Institutional Selectivity (N = 789)

	High (n = 113)	Other (n = 676)
Yes	54.0%	42.0%
No	46.0%	58.0%

$p < .05$

Table 4.11

Percentage of Institutions Reporting Team-Taught Sections by Institutional Size (N = 789)

	5,000 or less (n = 540)	5,001 – 10,000 (n = 123)	10,001 – 15,000 (n = 59)	15,001 - 20,000 (n = 32)	More than 20,000 (n = 35)
Frequency	224	58	27	19	17
Percentage	41.5	47.2	45.8	59.4	48.6

Table 4.12

Percentage of Institutions Reporting Team-Taught Sections by Seminar Type (N = 744)

	EO (n = 304)	AUC (n = 130)	AVC (n = 136)	BSS (n = 43)	PRE (n = 11)	Hybrid (n = 118)
Frequency	140	50	70	4	7	54
Percentage	46.1	38.5	51.5	9.3	63.6	45.8

Note. When *n* for seminar type < 10, data were omitted from the table.

$p < .05$

Table 4.13

Percentage of Students Enrolled in Team-Taught Sections Across All Institutions (N = 789)

Team-taught enrollment	Frequency	Percentage
100%	90	11.4
75 - 99%	23	2.9
50 - 74%	13	1.7
25 - 49%	22	2.8
Less than 25%	197	25.0
0%	444	56.3

Table 4.14
Percentage of Students Enrolled in Team-Taught Sections by Institutional Affiliation (N = 644)

Team-taught enrollment	Private (*n* = 342)	Public (*n* = 302)
100%	14.0	8.9
75 - 99%	2.1	4.0
50 - 74%	2.3	1.0
25 - 49%	3.5	3.0
Less than 25%	22.8	27.8
0%	55.3	55.3

Table 4.15
Percentage of Students Enrolled in Team-Taught Sections by Institutional Type (N = 776)

Team-taught enrollment	Two-year (*n* = 180)	Four-year (*n* = 596)
100%*	7.2	12.6
75 - 99%	1.1	3.5
50 - 74%	1.1	1.9
25 - 49%	1.7	3.0
Less than 25%	22.8	25.3
0%**	66.1	53.7

*$p < .05$. **$p < .01$.

Table 4.16
Percentage of Students Enrolled in Team-Taught Sections by Institutional Selectivity (N = 789)

Team-taught enrollment	High (*n* = 113)	Other (*n* = 676)
100%	10.6	11.5
75 - 99%	1.8	3.1
50 - 74%	2.7	1.5
25 - 49%	2.7	2.8
Less than 25%**	36.3	23.1
0%*	46.0	58.0

*$p < .05$. **$p < .01$.

Table 4.17

Percentage of Students Enrolled in Team-Taught Sections by Institutional Size (N = 789)

Team-taught enrollment	5,000 or less (*n* = 540)	5,001 - 10,000 (*n* = 123)	10,001 - 15,000 (*n* = 59)	15,001 – 20,000 (*n* = 32)	More than 20,000 (*n* = 35)
100%	13.2	9.8	6.8	9.4	0.0
75 - 99%	2.6	3.3	3.4	9.4	0.0
50 - 74%	1.9	0.0	1.7	3.1	2.9
25 - 49%	2.0	8.1	1.7	0.0	0.0
Less than 25%	21.9	26.0	32.2	37.5	45.7
0%	58.5	52.9	54.2	40.6	51.4

$p < .05$

Table 4.18

Percentage of Students Enrolled in Team-Taught Sections by Seminar Type (N = 744)

Team-taught enrollment	EO (*n* = 304)	AUC (*n* = 130)	AVC (*n* = 136)	BSS (*n* = 43)	PRE (*n* = 11)	Hybrid (*n* = 118)
100%	14.5	8.5	5.2	2.3	0.0	17.8
75 - 99%	3.3	2.3	1.5	0.0	0.0	1.7
50 - 74%	2.3	1.5	0.7	0.0	9.1	1.7
25 - 49%	2.0	5.4	3.7	0.0	9.1	2.5
Less than 25%	24.0	20.8	40.4	7.0	45.5	22.0
0%	54.0	61.5	48.5	90.7	36.4	54.2

Note. When *n* for seminar type < 10, data were omitted from the table.

$p < .05$

Instructors as Advisors

Only 31.9% of responding institutions placed students in sections taught by their academic advisors. Private institutions (40.2% vs. 23.4%) and highly selective schools (43.4% vs. 30.3%) were more likely to use academic advisors as instructors than their counterparts (Tables 4.19-4.24).

Table 4.19

Institutions With Sections Taught by Academic Advisor Across All Institutions (N = 802)

	Frequency	Percentage
Yes	256	31.9
No	546	68.1

Table 4.20

Institutions With Sections Taught by Academic Advisor by Institutional Affiliation (N = 651)

	Private (n = 343)	Public (n = 308)
Frequency	138	72
Percentage	40.2	23.4

$p < .05$

Table 4.21

Institutions With Sections Taught by Academic Advisor by Institutional Type (N = 789)

	Two-year (n = 183)	Four-year (n = 606)
Frequency	31	221
Percentage	16.9	36.5

$p < .05$

Table 4.22

Institutions With Sections Taught by Academic Advisor by Institutional Selectivity (N = 802)

	High (n = 113)	Other (n = 689)
Frequency	49	207
Percentage	43.4	30.3

$p < .05$

Table 4.23

Institutions With Sections Taught by Academic Advisor by Institutional Size (N = 802)

	5,000 or less (n = 549)	5,001 - 10,000 (n = 126)	10,001 - 15,000 (n = 60)	15,001 - 20,000 (n = 32)	More than 20,000 (n = 35)
Frequency	196	32	14	9	5
Percentage	35.7	25.4	23.3	28.1	14.3

$p < .05$

Table 4.24

Institutions With Sections Taught by Academic Advisor by Seminar Type (N = 758)

	EO (n = 313)	AUC (n = 129)	AVC (n = 137)	BSS (n = 43)	PRE (n = 12)	Hybrid (n = 122)
Frequency	89	45	55	6	3	39
Percentage	28.4	34.9	40.2	14.0	25.0	32.0

Note. When n for seminar type < 10, data were omitted from the table.

$p < .05$

Teaching Workload and Compensation

The remuneration for teaching the course varies greatly depending on position, experience, credit hours, and a host of other factors. Responding institutions that employ faculty as seminar instructors often considered the course as part of the regular teaching load (64.4%). When the course was not part of the regular load, participating institutions noted that teaching the course may be an overload or voluntary. The majority of highly selective and less selective schools reported that teaching the seminar was part of the regular teaching load for faculty, but less selective schools were more likely to report that faculty taught the course as an overload course (40.2% vs. 22.2%). For staff, teaching a seminar was an extra responsibility at 42.5% of the responding institutions, an assigned responsibility at 30.7% of the participating institutions, or "other" (6.2%).

Instructors received a stipend at 50.7% of the responding institutions. Some mentioned the stipend was given to faculty as travel funds, but most survey participants did not make this distinction so we assume the funds were given directly to faculty as additional salary. Private institutions were more likely than public ones to compensate instructors with a stipend (55.8% vs. 46.5%), but public institutions were more likely to offer some form of compensation other than a stipend, release time, or graduate student support (15.8% vs. 8.3%) (Tables 4.25-4.44).

Some respondents mentioned that the stipend amount varied based on faculty rank or credit hours but did not offer specific monetary figures. However, 370 participating institutions noted the stipend amount. Of those institutions, there was a wide range in the stipend amount from a low of $50 to a high of $7,500, with a mean of $1,498 and modal figure of $1,000 (36 institutions paid this amount).

A few respondents indicated that instructors got release time (5.5%) rather than a stipend for teaching the seminar as an extra responsibility or overload. At Allegheny College and SUNY-Geneseo, the instructor received a course release after teaching three semesters of the seminar. Some instructors got time off while they taught. At the University of Colorado, Colorado Springs, instructors received three hours of release time a week. Other institutions excused the instructors from work during the actual class time (e.g., Finlandia University). At McHenry County College, instructors got vacation days. These examples show that institutions are creative in how they offer remuneration to seminar instructors.

Table 4.25

Faculty Workload Configuration Across All Institutions (*N* = 821)

Seminar taught as	Frequency	Percentage
Part of regular teaching load	529	64.4
Overload course	309	37.6
Other	85	10.4

Note. Percentages do not equal 100%. Respondents could make more than one selection.

Table 4.26

Faculty Workload Configuration by Institutional Affiliation (*N* = 670)

Seminar taught as	Private (*n* = 351)	Public (*n* = 319)
Part of regular teaching load	64.1%	63.0%
Overload course	35.9%	40.8%
Other	12.5%	9.4%

Note. Percentages do not equal 100%. Respondents could make more than one selection.

Table 4.27

Faculty Workload Configuration by Institutional Type (*N* = 815)

Seminar taught as	Two-year (*n* = 196)	Four-year (*n* = 619)
Part of regular teaching load*	72.4%	62.2%
Overload course	35.2%	38.3%
Other	8.2%	11.0%

Note. Percentages do not equal 100%. Respondents could make more than one selection.
*$p < .05$

Table 4.28

Faculty Workload Configuration by Institutional Selectivity (*N* = 816)

Seminar taught as	High (*n* = 117)	Other (*n* = 699)
Part of regular teaching load	69.2%	63.7%
Overload course*	22.2%	40.2%
Other	10.3%	10.3%

Note. Percentages do not equal 100%. Respondents could make more than one selection.
*$p < .01$

Table 4.29
Faculty Workload Configuration by Institutional Size (*N* = 810)

Seminar taught as	5,000 or less (*n* = 553)	5,001 - 10,000 (*n* = 128)	10,001 - 15,000 (*n* = 60)	15,001 - 20,000 (*n* = 34)	More than 20,000 (*n* = 35)
Part of regular teaching load*	47.2%	67.2%	70.0%	44.1%	51.4%
Overload course	42.1%	38.3%	46.7%	50.0%	45.7%
Other	13.2%	10.9%	6.7%	14.7%	11.4%

Note. Percentages do not equal 100%. Respondents could make more than one selection.
*$p < .05$

Table 4.30
Faculty Workload Configuration by Seminar Type (*N* = 772)

Seminar taught as	EO (*n* = 316)	AUC (*n* = 134)	AVC (*n* = 138)	BSS (*n* = 45)	PRE (*n* = 12)	Hybrid (*n* = 125)
Part of regular teaching load*	49.7%	77.6%	83.3%	80.0%	83.3%	64.8%
Overload course*	34.5%	25.4%	18.8%	37.8%	25.0%	36.8%
Other	7.6%	3.7%	6.5%	6.7%	0.0%	5.6%

Note. Percentages do not equal 100%. Respondents could make more than one selection.
When *n* for seminar type < 10, data were omitted from the table.
*$p < .05$

Table 4.31
Administrative Staff Workload Configuration Across All Institutions (*N* = 821)

Seminar taught as	Frequency	Percentage
Assigned responsibility	252	30.7
Extra responsibility	349	42.5
Other	51	6.2

Table 4.32
Administrative Staff Workload Configuration by Institutional Affiliation (*N* = 667)

Seminar taught as	Private (*n* = 351)	Public (*n* = 316)
Assigned responsibility	26.5%	31.7%
Extra responsibility	43.3%	44.9%
Other	4.6%	8.5%

Table 4.33
Administrative Staff Workload Configuration by Institutional Type (N = 807)

Seminar taught as	Two-year (*n* = 188)	Four-year (*n* = 619)
Assigned responsibility*	36.7%	29.1%
Extra responsibility	37.8%	43.8%
Other	6.4%	6.1%

*p < .05

Table 4.34
Administrative Staff Workload Configuration by Institutional Selectivity (N = 821)

Seminar taught as	High (*n* = 117)	Other (*n* = 704)
Assigned responsibility*	18.0%	32.8%
Extra responsibility*	33.3%	44.0%
Other	5.1%	6.4%

*p < .01

Table 4.35
Administrative Staff Workload Configuration by Institutional Size (N = 821)

Seminar taught as	5,000 or less (*n* = 560)	5,001 - 10,000 (*n* = 129)	10,001 - 15,000 (*n* = 61)	15,001 - 20,000 (*n* = 35)	More than 20,000 (*n* = 36)
Assigned responsibility	28.6%	38.8%	37.7%	34.3%	19.4%
Extra responsibility	41.6%	43.4%	50.8%	37.1%	44.4%
Other*	5.2%	5.4%	6.6%	22.9%	8.3%

*p < .05

Table 4.36
Administrative Staff Workload Configuration by Seminar Type (N = 772)

Seminar taught as	EO (*n* = 316)	AUC (*n* = 134)	AVC (*n* = 138)	BSS (*n* = 45)	PRE (*n* = 12)	Hybrid (*n* = 125)
Assigned responsibility*	34.5%	25.4%	18.8%	37.8%	25.0%	36.8%
Extra responsibility*	53.2%	39.6%	32.6%	28.9%	33.3%	38.4%
Other	7.6%	3.7%	6.5%	6.7%	0.0%	5.6%

Note. When *n* for seminar type < 10, data were omitted from the table.
*p < .05

Table 4.37

Instructor Compensation Across All Institutions (*N* = 821)

Compensation type	Frequency	Percentage
Stipend	416	50.7
Release time	45	5.5
Graduate student support	8	1.0
Other	96	11.7

Table 4.38

Instructor Compensation by Institutional Affiliation (*N* = 667)

Compensation type	Private (*n* = 351)	Public (*n* = 316)
Stipend*	55.8%	46.5%
Release time	4.6%	7.6%
Graduate student support	0.3%	1.6%
Other**	8.3%	15.8%

*p < .05. **p < .01.

Table 4.39

Instructor Compensation by Institutional Type (*N* = 807)

Compensation type	Two-year (*n* = 188)	Four-year (*n* = 619)
Stipend**	37.2%	54.9%
Release time	3.7%	6.1%
Graduate student support	0.0%	1.3%
Other**	17.6%	9.7%

**p < .01

Table 4.40

Instructor Compensation by Institutional Selectivity (*N* = 821)

Compensation type	High (*n* = 117)	Other (*n* = 704)
Stipend*	41.0%	52.3%
Release time	7.7%	5.1%
Graduate student support	0.9%	1.0%
Other	6.8%	12.5%

*p < .05

Table 4.41

Instructor Compensation by Institutional Size (*N* = 821)

Compensation type	5,000 or less (*n* = 560)	5,001 - 10,000 (*n* = 129)	10,001 - 15,000 (*n* = 61)	15,001 - 20,000 (*n* = 35)	More than 20,000 (*n* = 36)
Stipend*	53.9%	44.2%	45.9%	48.6%	33.3%
Release time*	4.6%	8.5%	3.3%	0.0%	16.7%
Graduate student support	0.5%	1.6%	1.6%	2.9%	2.8%
*Other	9.1%	13.2%	18.0%	22.9%	25.0%

*p < .05

Table 4.42

Instructor Compensation by Seminar Type (*N* = 772)

Compensation type	EO (*n* = 316)	AUC (*n* = 134)	AVC (*n* = 138)	BSS (*n* = 45)	PRE (*n* = 12)	Hybrid (*n* = 125)
Stipend*	57.6%	56.0%	44.9%	26.7%	41.7%	44.8%
Release time*	3.8%	3.0%	8.7%	2.2%	8.3%	7.2%
Graduate student support	1.6%	0.8%	1.5%	0.0%	0.0%	0.0%
Other	14.6%	8.2%	8.7%	15.6%	16.7%	12.0%

Note. When *n* for seminar type < 10, data were omitted from the table.

*p < .05

Table 4.43

Faculty Workload Configuration by Instructor Compensation (*N* = 565)

Seminar taught as	Compensation			
	Stipend (*n* = 416)	Release time (*n* = 45)	Graduate student support (*n* = 8)	Other (*n* = 96)
Part of regular teaching load**	54.3%	75.6%	50.0%	55.2%
Overload course*	60.6%	55.6%	50.0%	51.0%
Other**	8.9%	8.9%	0.0%	28.1%

*p < .05. ***p* < .01.

Table 4.44

Administrative Staff Workload Configuration by Instructor Compensation (N = 565)

	Compensation			
Seminar taught as	**Stipend** **(n = 416)**	**Release time** **(n = 45)**	**Graduate student support** **(n = 8)**	**Other** **(n = 96)**
Assigned responsibility*	25.5%	26.7%	62.5%	30.2%
Extra responsibility**	66.8%	46.7%	37.5%	50.0%
Other**	5.0%	6.7%	30.2%	21.9%

*$p < .05$. **$p < .01$.

Instructor Training

More than three fourths (76.8%) of institutions reported that they *offered* instructor training, but approximately 50% *required* instructor training. More than 60% of reporting two-year institutions and 81.1% of four-year institutions indicated that they offer instructor training to first-year seminar instructors. Similarly, fewer two-year institutions required their instructors to complete training than at four-year schools (39.6% vs. 56%). Less-selective institutions were more likely to require training than highly selective institutions (54.5% vs. 38.4%). Most training sessions were one day or less, with 35.4% lasting half a day or less and 24.3% lasting one day. At both two-year and four-year institutions, training was most often offered for a half day or less (51.8% at two-year schools vs. 31.4% at four-year schools) (Tables 4.45-4.62).

Table 4.45

Instructor Training Offered Across All Institutions (N = 797)

	Frequency	**Percentage**
Yes	612	76.8
No	185	23.2

Table 4.46

Instructor Training Offered by Institutional Affiliation (N = 651)

	Private **(n = 345)**	**Public** **(n = 306)**
Frequency	278	228
Percentage	80.6	74.5

Table 4.47
Instructor Training Offered by Institutional Type (*N* = 783)

	Two-year (*n* = 179)	**Four-year** (*n* = 604)
Frequency	111	490
Percentage	62.0	81.1

p < .01

Table 4.48
Instructor Training Offered by Institutional Selectivity (*N* = 797)

	High (*n* = 112)	**Other** (*n* = 685)
Frequency	91	521
Percentage	81.2	76.1

Table 4.49
Instructor Training Offered by Institutional Size (*N* = 797)

	5,000 or less (*n* = 545)	**5,001 - 10,000** (*n* = 125)	**10,001 - 15,000** (*n* = 59)	**15,001 - 20,000** (*n* = 33)	**More than 20,000** (*n* = 35)
Frequency	412	92	50	28	30
Percentage	75.6	73.6	84.8	84.9	85.7

Table 4.50
Instructor Training Offered by Seminar Type (*N* = 753)

	EO (*n* = 310)	**AUC** (*n* = 130)	**AVC** (*n* = 136)	**BSS** (*n* = 42)	**PRE** (*n* = 11)	**Hybrid** (*n* = 122)
Frequency	243	104	111	18	8	91
Percentage	78.4	80.0	81.6	42.9	72.7	74.6

Note. When *n* for seminar type < 10, data were omitted from the table.
p < .05

Table 4.51
Instructor Training Required Across All Institutions (*N* = 796)

	Frequency	**Percentage**
Yes	416	52.3
No	380	47.7

Table 4.52
Instructor Training Required by Institutional Affiliation (*N* = 646)

	Private (*n* = 342)	Public (*n* = 304)
Frequency	194	150
Percentage	56.7	49.3

Table 4.53
Instructor Training Required by Institutional Type (*N* = 782)

	Two-year (*n* = 182)	Four-year (*n* = 600)
Frequency	72	336
Percentage	39.6	56.0

$p < .01$

Table 4.54
Instructor Training Required by Institutional Selectivity (*N* = 796)

	High (*n* = 112)	Other (*n* = 684)
Frequency	43	373
Percentage	38.4	54.5

$p < .05$

Table 4.55
Instructor Training Required by Institutional Size (*N* = 796)

	5,000 or less (*n* = 542)	5,001 - 10,000 (*n* = 126)	10,001 - 15,000 (*n* = 59)	15,001 - 20,000 (*n* = 34)	More than 20,000 (*n* = 35)
Frequency	284	61	32	23	16
Percentage	52.4	48.4	54.2	67.7	45.7

Table 4.56
Instructor Training Required by Seminar Type (*N* = 751)

	EO (*n* = 308)	AUC (*n* = 128)	AVC (*n* = 137)	BSS (*n* = 44)	PRE (*n* = 12)	Hybrid (*n* = 120)
Frequency	174	76	62	12	3	61
Percentage	56.5	59.4	45.3	27.3	25.0	50.8

Note. When *n* for seminar type < 10, data were omitted from the table.
$p < .05$

Table 4.57
Length of Instructor Training Across All Institutions (*N* = 596)

Length of training	Frequency	Percentage
Half day or less	211	35.4
One day	145	24.3
Two days	80	13.4
Three days	31	5.2
Four days	10	1.7
One week	14	2.4
Other	105	17.6

Table 4.58
Length of Instructor Training by Institutional Affiliation (*N* = 495)

Length of training	Private (*n* = 271)	Public (*n* = 224)
Half day or less	36.5%	37.1%
One day	24.3%	25.0%
Two days	12.2%	13.8%
Three days	4.4%	4.0%
Four days	2.6%	0.9%
One week	3.0%	1.8%
Other	17.0%	17.4%

Table 4.59
Length of Instructor Training by Institutional Type (*N* = 585)

Length of training	Two-year (*n* = 110)	Four-year (*n* = 475)
Half day or less**	51.8%	31.4%
One day	20.0%	25.7%
Two days	8.2%	14.3%
Three days	2.7%	5.7%
Four days	1.8%	1.7%
One week	0.9%	2.7%
Other	14.6%	18.5%

**$p < .01$

Table 4.60

Length of Instructor Training by Institutional Selectivity (*N* = 596)

Length of training	High (*n* = 88)	Other (*n* = 508)
Half day or less	30.7%	36.2%
One day	25.0%	24.2%
Two days	12.5%	13.6%
Three days	8.0%	4.7%
Four days	3.4%	1.4%
One week	4.6%	2.0%
Other	15.9%	17.9%

Table 4.61

Length of Instructor Training by Institutional Size (*N* = 596)

Length of training	5,000 or less (*n* = 398)	5,001 - 10,000 (*n* = 90)	10,001 - 15,000 (*n* = 50)	15,001 - 20,000 (*n* = 28)	More than 20,000 (*n* = 30)
Half day or less	36.4%	42.2%	34.0%	14.3%	23.3%
One day	24.4%	17.8%	34.0%	21.4%	30.0%
Two days	13.1%	13.3%	6.0%	25.0%	20.0%
Three days	5.5%	3.3%	4.0%	10.7%	3.3%
Four days	2.0%	2.2%	0.0%	0.0%	0.0%
One week	2.8%	2.2%	2.0%	0.0%	0.0%
Other	15.8%	18.9%	20.0%	28.6%	23.3%

Table 4.62
Length of Instructor Training by Seminar Type (*N* = 561)

Length of training	EO (*n* = 238)	AUC (*n* = 100)	AVC (*n* = 107)	BSS (*n* = 17)	PRE (*n* = 8)	Hybrid (*n* = 89)
Half day or less	41.2%	29.0%	30.8%	29.4%	37.5%	32.6%
One day	26.9%	22.0%	26.2%	17.7%	25.0%	20.2%
Two days	10.9%	13.0%	16.8%	11.8%	0.0%	14.6%
Three days	2.9%	5.0%	9.4%	5.9%	0.0%	6.7%
Four days	1.7%	4.0%	0.0%	0.0%	0.0%	1.1%
One week	1.7%	4.0%	1.9%	0.0%	12.5%	3.4%
Other	14.7%	23.0%	15.0%	35.3%	25.0%	21.4%

Note. When *n* for seminar type < 10, data were omitted from the table.

Conclusion

In this chapter, we include a wide range of details regarding the instruction of first-year seminars including who is responsible for seminar instruction, team teaching configurations, workload and compensation, and instructor training. Faculty were used more frequently to teach the seminar at all types of institutions. Though training is frequently available, it tended to be brief (half day or less) and not necessarily required. The next chapter focuses on first-year seminar assessment practices.

Chapter 5

Course Objectives and Assessment

Angela Griffin and Barbara F. Tobolowsky

This chapter focuses on course assessment including information about the nature of the seminar assessment, methods employed, and findings from that assessment as reported by the participating institutions. Because identifying course objectives is so closely aligned with assessment, the chapter begins with details regarding the most common course objectives. As in previous chapters, the data are reported by institutional type, affiliation, selectivity, size, and type of seminar.

Course Objectives

Survey respondents were asked to select the three most important seminar objectives. The two most frequently selected objectives were to develop academic skills (64.2%) and orient students to campus resources and services (52.9%). A significant number of respondents also selected encouraging self-exploration and personal development (36.9%) and creating a common first-year experience (35.9%) as primary objectives.

Both two- and four-year institutions indicated that the most important course objectives for their seminars were developing academic skills (66.5% at two-year institutions vs. 64.0% at four-year institutions) and providing orientation to campus resources (71.3% at two-year institutions and 46.9% at four-year institutions). However, the most important course objectives varied by institutional affiliation, selectivity, and seminar type.

Public and less selective institutions were more likely to report orienting students to campus resources and services, encouraging self-exploration and personal development, and developing a support network and friendships as important course objectives. Conversely, private institutions were more likely to report creating a common first-year experience as the most important seminar objective. In addition, highly selective institutions were more likely to indicate goals of increasing student-faculty interaction and introducing a discipline than less selective schools (Tables 5.1-5.6).

Table 5.1

Most Important Course Objectives Across All Institutions (N = 821)

Course objective	Frequency	Percentage
Develop academic skills	527	64.2
Orient to campus resources & services	434	52.9
Encourage self-exploration/ personal development	303	36.9
Create common first-year experience	295	35.9
Develop support network/friendships	265	32.3
Increase student/faculty interaction	250	30.5
Improve sophomore return rates	205	25.0
Introduce a discipline	71	8.7
Encourage arts participation	11	1.3
Other	86	10.5

Note. Percentages do not equal 100%. Respondents were asked to select three most important objectives.

Table 5.2

Most Important Course Objectives by Institutional Affiliation (N = 667)

Course objective	Private (n = 351)	Public (n = 316)
Develop academic skills	60.7%	64.2%
Orient to campus resources & services*	40.7%	65.2%
Encourage self-exploration personal development*	33.9%	39.9%
Create common first-year experience*	47.0%	23.4%
Develop support network/friendships*	30.8%	35.4%
Increase student/faculty interaction*	35.0%	27.5%
Improve sophomore return rates	23.9%	25.0%
Introduce a discipline	7.7%	11.1%
Encourage arts participation	2.0%	0.3%
Other*	14.3%	7.3%

Note. Percentages do not equal 100%. Respondents were asked to select three most important objectives.
*$p < .05$

Table 5.3

Most Important Course Objectives by Institutional Type (N = 807)

Course objective	Two-Year (n = 188)	Four-Year (n = 619)
Develop academic skills	66.5%	64.0%
Orient to campus resources & services*	71.3%	46.9%
Encourage self-exploration/ personal development*	53.7%	31.8%
Create common first-year experience*	23.4%	39.7%
Develop support network/friendships	34.0%	31.2%
Increase student/faculty interaction*	16.5%	35.1%
Improve sophomore return rates	25.5%	25.0%
Introduce a discipline*	2.7%	10.0%
Encourage arts participation	1.6%	1.3%
Other*	4.3%	12.4%

Note. Percentages do not equal 100%. Respondents were asked to select three most important objectives.
*p < .05

Table 5.4

Most Important Course Objectives by Institutional Selectivity (N = 821)

Course objective	High (n = 117)	Other (n = 704)
Develop academic skills	67.5%	63.6%
Orient to campus resources and services*	23.1%	57.8%
Encourage self-exploration/ personal development*	21.4%	39.5%
Create common first-year experience	40.2%	35.2%
Develop support network/friendships*	24.8%	33.5%
Increase student/faculty interaction*	49.6%	27.3%
Improve sophomore return rates*	12.8%	27.0%
Introduce a discipline*	18.8%	7.0%
Encourage arts participation	0.0%	1.6%
Other*	21.4%	8.7%

Note. Percentages do not equal 100%. Respondents were asked to select three most important objectives.
*p < .05

Table 5.5

Most Important Course Objectives by Institutional Size (N = 821)

Course objective	5,000 or less (n = 560)	5,001 - 10,000 (n = 129)	10,001 - 15,000 (n = 61)	15,001 - 20,000 (n = 35)	More than 20,000 (n = 36)
Develop academic skills	63.8%	62.8%	62.3%	77.1%	66.7%
Orient to campus resources & services*	50.2%	55.0%	72.1%	60.0%	47.2%
Encourage self-exploration/ personal development	37.3%	38.0%	37.7%	34.3%	27.8%
Create common first-year experience*	40.5%	28.7%	29.5%	17.1%	19.4%
Develop support network/friendships	32.1%	32.6%	31.2%	25.7%	41.7%
Increase student/ faculty interaction	29.3%	36.4%	24.6%	20.0%	47.2%
Improve sophomore return rates	23.9%	32.6%	21.3%	22.9%	22.2%
Introduce a discipline*	6.4%	17.1%	6.6%	11.4%	13.9%
Encourage arts participation	1.8%	0.8%	0.0%	0.0%	0.0%
Other	11.1%	8.5%	4.9%	17.1%	11.1%

Note. Percentages do not equal 100%. Respondents were asked to select three most important objectives.
*$p < .05$

Table 5.6

Most Important Course Objectives by Seminar Type (*N* = 772)

Course objective	EO (*n* = 316)	AUC (*n* = 134)	AVC (*n* = 138)	BSS (*n* = 45)	PRE (*n* = 12)	Hybrid (*n* = 125)
Develop academic skills*	56.0%	71.6%	75.4%	82.2%	67.7%	60.0%
Orient to campus resources & services*	78.2%	29.1%	23.2%	53.3%	41.7%	48.8%
Encourage self-exploration /personal development*	46.5%	29.1%	16.7%	51.1%	41.7%	39.2%
Create common first-year experience*	27.9%	59.7%	37.7%	22.2%	50.0%	28.0%
Develop support network/friendships*	38.9%	29.9%	21.0%	28.9%	33.3%	32.0%
Increase student/ faculty interaction*	20.6%	28.4%	63.8%	15.6%	33.3%	26.4%
Improve sophomore return rates	25.6%	25.4%	26.1%	26.7%	8.3%	24.0%
Introduce a discipline*	2.9%	8.2%	15.9%	2.2%	50.0%	14.4%
Encourage arts participation	1.3%	0.8%	2.2%	0.0%	8.3%	0.8%
Other*	3.5%	17.9%	18.1%	4.4%	8.3%	16.8%

Note. Percentages do not equal 100%. Respondents were asked to select three most important objectives. When *n* for seminar type < 10, data were omitted from the table.

*p < .05

Assessment Methods

Once course goals have been identified, institutions must design methods for assessing the seminar's effectiveness in these areas. The survey asked a set of questions about the institutional assessment of first-year seminars. Only 60.2% of all participating institutions stated that they had done a formal assessment or evaluation of their seminar since 2003. Student course evaluations were the most common form of assessment, but other methods were used as well. If institutions used a survey instrument, most respondents created their own (88.7%), although more than half noted using an external instrument (57.7%). Institutions mentioned using Your First College Year (YFCY), National Survey of Student Engagement (NSSE), Community College Survey of Student Engagement (CCSSE), First-Year Initiative (FYI), and the Student Satisfaction Inventory (SSI) surveys among others. Tables 5.7 through 5.12 highlight the details of seminar assessments.

Table 5.7

Types of Evaluation Methods Across All Institutions (N = 821)

Evaluation method	Number of institutions	Percentage
Instructor focus groups	242	63.5
Student focus groups	187	51.2
Instructor interviews	185	53.6
Student interviews	119	36.8
Course evaluations	457	97.2
Survey instruments	342	82.4
Institutional data	300	79.2

Note. Percentages do not equal 100%. Respondents could make more than one selection.

Table 5.8

Types of Evaluation Methods by Institutional Affiliation

Evaluation method	Private	Public
Instructor focus groups	(*n* = 174) 67.2%	(*n* = 142) 63.4%
Student focus groups	(*n* = 167) 50.9%	(*n* = 134) 51.5%
Instructor interviews	(*n* = 157) 54.8%	(*n* = 130) 55.4%
Student interviews	(*n* = 62) 36.1%	(*n* = 256) 35.3%
Course evaluations	(*n* = 218) 97.3%	(*n* = 169) 98.8%
Survey instruments	(*n* = 193) 81.4%	(*n* = 151) 84.1%
Institutional data	(*n* = 168) 75.0%	(*n* = 145) 82.8%

Note. Percentages do not equal 100%. Respondents could make more than one selection.

Table 5.9

Types of Evaluation Methods by Institutional Type

Evaluation method	Two-year	Four-year
Instructor focus groups	(*n* = 74) 56.8%	(*n* = 300) 64.7%
Student focus groups	(*n* = 70) 42.9%	(*n* = 289) 52.9%
Instructor interviews	(*n* = 65) 55.4%	(*n* = 274) 52.9%
Student interviews	(*n* = 62) 32.3%	(*n* = 256) 37.9%
Course evaluation	(*n* = 87) 95.4%	(*n* = 376) 97.6%
Survey instruments*	(*n* = 78) 73.1%	(*n* = 331) 84.6%
Institutional data	(*n* = 73) 83.6%	(*n* = 300) 78.3%

Note. Percentages do not equal 100%. Respondents could make more than one selection.
*$p < .05$

Table 5.10

Types of Evaluation Methods by Institutional Selectivity

Evaluation method	High	Other
Instructor focus groups	(*n* = 48) 62.5%	(*n* = 333) 63.7%
Student focus groups	(*n* = 48) 50.0%	(*n* = 317) 51.4%
Instructor interviews	(*n* = 43) 51.2%	(*n* = 302) 54.0%
Student interviews	(*n* = 41) 34.2%	(*n* = 282) 37.2%
Course evaluations	(*n* = 63) 96.8%	(*n* = 407) 97.3%
Survey instruments	(*n* = 56) 89.3%	(*n* = 359) 81.3%
Institutional data	(*n* = 52) 76.9%	(*n* = 327) 79.5%

Note. Percentages do not equal 100%. Respondents could make more than one selection.

Table 5.11

Types of Evaluation Methods by Institutional Size

Evaluation method	5,000 or less	5,001 - 10,000	10,001 - 15,000	15,001 - 20,000	More than 20,000
Instructor focus groups	(n = 262) 64.1%	(n = 48) 70.8%	(n = 31) 54.8%	(n = 20) 55.0%	(n = 20) 60.0%
Student focus groups	(n = 123) 49.0%	(n = 30) 61.2%	(n = 14) 48.3%	(n = 17) 41.2%	(n = 13) 68.4%
Instructor interviews	(n = 124) 52.1%	(n = 27) 62.8%	(n = 13) 46.4%	(n = 9) 52.9%	(n = 12) 63.2%
Student interviews	(n = 84) 37.2%	(n = 16) 42.1%	(n = 10) 38.5%	(n = 5) 31.3%	(n = 4) 23.5%
Course evaluations	(n = 317) 96.9%	(n = 60) 98.4%	(n = 34) 97.1%	(n = 24) 100.0%	(n = 22) 95.7%
Survey instruments	(n = 230) 80.7%	(n = 46) 85.2%	(n = 30) 85.7%	(n = 19) 86.4%	(n = 17) 89.5%
Institutional data	(n = 191) 76.7%	(n = 49) 89.1%	(n = 27) 87.1%	(n = 18) 81.2%	(n = 15) 68.2%

Note. Percentages do not equal 100%. Respondents could make more than one selection.

Table 5.12

Types of Evaluation Methods by Seminar Type

Evaluation method	EO	AUC	AVC	BSS	Hybrid
Instructor focus groups	(n = 156) 63.5%	(n = 58) 60.3%	(n = 58) 63.8%	(n = 17) 35.3%	(n = 65) 69.2%
Student focus groups	(n = 149) 47.7%	(n = 59) 64.4%	(n = 52) 53.9%	(n = 16) 25.0%	(n = 64) 51.6%
Instructor interviews	(n = 144) 52.8%	(n = 51) 58.8%	(n = 49) 57.1%	(n = 15) 40.0%	(n = 65) 53.9%
Student interviews	(n = 134) 35.8%	(n = 46) 37.0%	(n = 48) 37.5%	(n = 15) 13.3%	(n = 60) 43.3%
Course evaluations	(n = 184) 97.3%	(n = 74) 98.7%	(n = 77) 98.7%	(n = 18) 83.3%	(n = 82) 97.6%
Survey instruments	(n = 170) 81.7%	(n = 65) 84.6%	(n = 68) 89.7%	(n = 17) 52.9%	(n = 68) 77.9%
Institutional data	(n = 148) 73.7%	(n = 58) 86.2%	(n = 60) 83.3%	(n = 18) 83.3%	(n = 66) 77.3%

Note. Percentages do not equal 100%. Respondents could make more than one selection.
When n for seminar type < 10, data were omitted from the table.

Assessment Findings

The 2006 national survey asked respondents if their assessments revealed that selected outcomes were improved or increased. Across all seminar types, increased persistence to the sophomore year (43.4%) and improved student connections with peers (41.2%) were the most likely variables to be measured and found. It must be noted that because of the wording of the question only those institutions that had both assessed the particular outcome *and* found an improvement would have selected a specific response. Schools were left out of this analysis if they had not done related assessment and/or if their assessment did not indicate improvement in a particular area. In addition, a number of institutions required all students to enroll in the seminar, making it impossible to measure increases or decreases in outcomes because no control group was available for comparison. For all these reasons, we advise caution in interpreting and communicating these findings (Tables 5.13-5.18).

Table 5.13
Results Attributed to First-Year Seminar Across All Institutions (N =488)

Seminar improved or increased	Number of institutions	Percentage
Persistence to sophomore year	212	43.4
Student connection with peers	201	41.2
Student satisfaction with the institution	186	38.1
Student use of campus services	165	33.8
Out-of-class student/faculty interaction	165	33.8
Level of student participation in campus activities	158	32.4
Student satisfaction with faculty	147	30.1
Academic abilities	142	29.1
Persistence to graduation	87	17.8
Grade point average	86	17.6
Other	88	18.0

Note. Percentages do not equal 100%. Respondents were able to make more than one selection.

Table 5.14

Results Attributed to First-Year Seminars by Institutional Affiliation (*N* = 404)

Seminar improved or increased	Private (*n* = 231)	Public (*n* = 173)
Persistence to sophomore year*	34.2%	53.8%
Student connection with peers	37.7%	45.7%
Student use of campus services	33.3%	36.4%
Out-of-class student/faculty interaction	36.8%	30.1%
Level of student participation in campus activities	31.2%	34.1%
Student satisfaction with the institution	36.8%	39.3%
Student satisfaction with faculty	32.5%	24.3%
Academic abilities	27.3%	28.9%
Persistence to graduation*	11.7%	21.4%
Grade point average*	6.5%	28.9%
Other	17.3%	19.7%

Note. Percentages do not equal 100%. Respondents were able to make more than one selection.
*p < .05

Table 5.15

Results Attributed to First-Year Seminars by Institutional Type (*N* = 481)

Seminar improved or increased	Two-year (*n* = 90)	Four-year (*n* = 391)
Persistence to sophomore year	48.9%	42.2%
Student connection with peers	33.3%	43.0%
Student use of campus services*	43.3%	31.2%
Out-of-class student/faculty interaction	34.4%	34.0%
Level of student participation in campus activities	32.2%	32.2%
Student satisfaction with the institution	41.1%	37.1%
Student satisfaction with faculty*	21.1%	32.2%
Academic abilities	36.7%	27.4%
Persistence to graduation*	30.0%	15.1%
Grade point average*	27.8%	15.6%
Other	14.4%	18.7%

Note. Percentages do not equal 100%. Respondents were able to make more than one selection.
*p < .05

Table 5.16

Results Attributed to First-Year Seminars by Institutional Selectivity (*N* = 488)

Seminar improved or increased	High (*n* = 65)	Other (*n* = 423)
Persistence to sophomore year*	24.6%	46.3%
Student connection with peers	41.4%	41.1%
Student use of campus services*	13.9%	36.9%
Out-of-class student/faculty interaction	33.9%	33.8%
Level of student participation in campus activities*	18.5%	34.5%
Student satisfaction with the institution	41.5%	37.6%
Student satisfaction with faculty*	44.6%	27.9%
Academic abilities	35.4%	28.1%
Persistence to graduation	13.9%	18.4%
Grade point average*	4.6%	19.6%
Other*	29.2%	16.3%

Note. Percentages do not equal 100%. Respondents were able to make more than one selection.

*$p < .05$

Table 5.17

Results Attributed to First-Year Seminar by Institutional Size ($N = 488$)

Seminar improved or increased	5,000 or less ($n = 343$)	5,001 - 10,000 ($n = 62$)	10,001 - 15,000 ($n = 36$)	15,001 - 20,000 ($n = 24$)	More than 20,000 ($n = 23$)
Persistence to sophomore year*	38.2%	54.8%	47.2%	79.2%	47.8%
Student connection with peers	39.4%	46.8%	30.6%	58.3%	52.2%
Student use of campus services	35.6%	27.4%	30.6%	29.2%	34.8%
Out-of-class student/ faculty interaction	36.2%	33.9%	16.7%	20.8%	39.1%
Level of student participation in campus activities	32.7%	37.1%	16.7%	37.5%	34.8%
Student satisfaction with the institution	37.0%	40.3%	41.7%	45.8%	34.8%
Student satisfaction with faculty	31.5%	21.0%	25.0%	37.5%	34.8%
Academic abilities	27.7%	35.5%	30.6%	37.5%	21.7%
Persistence to graduation	15.5%	22.6%	25.0%	25.0%	21.7%
Grade point average*	9.9%	29.0%	38.9%	54.2%	30.4%
Other	16.9%	24.2%	25.0%	12.5%	13.0%

Note. Percentages do not equal 100%. Respondents were able to make more than one selection.

*$p < .05$

Table 5.18

Results Attributed to First-Year Seminar by Seminar Type (N = 458)

Seminar improved or increased	EO (n = 192)	AUC (n = 75)	AVC (n = 82)	BSS (n = 19)	Hybrid (n = 83)
Persistence to sophomore year*	50.5%	32.0%	34.2%	63.2%	45.8%
Student connection with peers*	44.8%	38.7%	41.5%	5.3%	42.2%
Student use of campus services*	42.7%	20.0%	20.7%	21.1%	33.7%
Out-of-class student/ faculty interaction	33.3%	34.7%	42.7%	15.8%	30.1%
Level of student participation in campus activities*	40.6%	34.7%	18.3%	21.1%	26.5%
Student satisfaction with the institution	43.2%	32.0%	35.4%	15.8%	41.0%
Student satisfaction with faculty*	25.0%	32.0%	39.0%	15.8%	31.3%
Academic abilities	26.0%	36.0%	32.9%	47.4%	30.1%
Persistence to graduation	18.8%	16.0%	13.4%	21.1%	13.3%
Grade point average	21.4%	10.7%	15.9%	31.6%	16.9%
Other	13.0%	22.7%	26.8%	10.5%	22.9%

Note. Percentages do not equal 100%. Respondents were able to make more than one selection.

When *n* for seminar type < 10, data were omitted from the table.

*$p < .05$

A number of institutions selected the "other" response and provided details regarding other outcomes that they measured. Some respondents summarized their findings based on research or anecdotal evidence because they were not currently conducting any type of formal assessment at the time of the 2006 survey administration. Included below are some of the other outcomes identified:

- "Increased ... student understanding of aims and goals of their college education" (Hendrix College)
- Exposure to new ideas from other students (UCLA)
- Improvement in critical thinking skills[1] (Loras College, Kalamazoo College)
- Improvement in writing (Kalamazoo College)
- Improved library skills (Plymouth State University)
- Fewer academic integrity issues and "greater levels of responsibility for those engaged in misconduct" (Austin College)
- "Increased coherence between different sections/instructors" (Carroll College)

Conclusion

Assessment remains a critical component in illustrating the value of the seminar. Yet, it is telling that only 60.2% of the institutions responded that they have conducted formal assessment of their seminar since 2003. It is essential that campuses invest the time to identify learning objectives and measure them to ensure both the ongoing relevance of the seminar and its very existence.

Another interesting point is that the range of outcomes reflects the idiosyncratic nature of variables. For example, "critical thinking skills" on one campus may be labeled as something else at another campus. Campuses, appropriately, link the variables to their specific learning objectives. Thus, the wording of a variable or outcome is very campus-specific, making it impossible to accurately report the frequencies of these measures. Nevertheless, it appears that outcomes are, on the whole, tied to institutional mission, improved connection to peers and faculty, skill acquisition, and retention.

Notes

[1]"Critical thinking skills" is different from "academic skills," which was a variable identified in the survey.

Chapter 6

Summary of Selected Findings

Barbara F. Tobolowsky

Since 1988, the goal of the National Survey on First-Year Seminars has been to provide a deeper understanding of the administration, instruction, and assessment of first-year seminars. This chapter provides an overview of key findings, including a trends analysis of survey results from that first survey in 1988 to the present. Our hope is that the snapshot presented in these pages will help institutions as they develop, improve, and/or institutionalize their seminars.

Selected Key Findings

The survey explored the seminar in terms of the course, the students, the instructors, and the course administration. Though this list is not exhaustive, it provides a portrait of the first-year seminar by sharing key findings in those same areas.

The Course[1]

- The most common type of seminar at reporting institutions is the extended orientation seminar (57.9%). However, 53.8% of the respondents offer some type of academic seminar (28.1% offer academic seminars with uniform content, and 25.7% offer academic seminars with variable content), which suggests the continuation of the increasing trend toward more academic seminars.
- Seminar classes tend to be small. The section size for approximately 85% of the respondents across all institutional types is between 10 to 25 students with 16 to 20 students per section being the most prevalent (36.9%). Seminars with an academic focus are more likely to be smaller than the other seminar types.
- The course at 92.2% of the responding institutions carries credit toward graduation.
- At private institutions, the course is more likely applied as general education credit; whereas, at public institutions, it is more likely to be applied as an elective credit according to our respondents.
- The course typically carries one credit (42.5% of responding institutions) or three credits (32.7% of responding institutions). Extended orientation type courses are more likely to carry one credit in comparison to all other seminar types.
- At most of the responding institutions, students receive a letter grade for the course (82%), with only 2.5% of participants stating their course offers no grade.

- More than 40% of responding institutions offer a service-learning component.
- Almost 35.3% of institutions offer the seminar as part of a first-year learning community.
- Respondents (across all institutional types) note that the most important objectives for their seminars are to develop academic skills (64.2%) and orient students to campus resources and services (52.9%).
- Respondents (across all institutional types) report that study skills (40.8%) and critical thinking (40.6%) are the most important course topics in their seminars.

The Students[2]

- The seminar is required for all students at 46% of the participating institutions, but 19.4% of the institutions do not require it of any of their first-year students.
- When the seminar is required for a special student population, it is most frequently required for provisionally admitted students (20.1%).
- However, special sections of the seminar are offered at more than 60% of the participating institutions and are most likely offered for honors students (22.4%) and academically underprepared students (19.9%).

The Instructors[3]

- At 90% of the institutions, faculty teach the first-year seminar. For most of the faculty, teaching the seminar is part of their regular teaching load (64.4%).
- At 72% of the participating institutions, student affairs or other campus professionals teach the seminar. For staff, the course is more likely to be an extra responsibility (42.5%).
- At 31.9% of responding institutions, academic advisors teach their advisees in the first-year seminar.
- Instructor training is offered at 76.8% of the responding institutions and required at 52.3% of them.
- Instructor training tends to last two days or less at 73.1% of the participating institutions, with it most commonly lasting half a day or less (35.4%).

The Administration[4]

- At almost 51% of the participating institutions, the seminar is housed in academic affairs, with the second largest percentage reporting that the seminar is housed in an academic department (13.5%).
- There is a dean/director/coordinator of the first-year seminar at almost 80% of the responding institutions. Almost two thirds of the respondents said that the dean/director/coordinator is less than full-time (62.1%), and 48.7% say that the coordinator/director's other responsibility is as faculty.
- Assessment is reported by 60.2% of the participating institutions (n = 488).[5]

Trends

Table 6.1 reflects the general response rate for the 2006 survey as it compares to previous administrations. This survey instrument has minor variations from the 2003 instrument but is dramatically different from the instruments used prior to that administration. Therefore, it is impossible to draw direct comparisons between the seminar results at each survey administration. However, it is possible to see trends from these snapshots among the responding institutions over the years.

Many of the findings are consistent over the seven survey administrations (Table 6.2). Some of those points of consistency are:

- *Seminar type.* Though there has been a decline in the participants that offer extended orientation seminars, this remains the most prevalent type of seminar.
- *Required status.* Seminars have been required by almost half of all participating institutions since 1988.
- *Credit.* More than 80% of all participating institutions have offered seminars for credit, although how that credit is applied has changed with different administrations.
- *Instruction.* Between 84-90% of the participating institutions have used faculty as instructors of the seminars.
- *Instructor training.* About three quarters of all participating institutions through the years have offered instructor training.

These areas of consistency reflect practices that appear to be integral to the seminar from its inception—small, required courses that have credit attached, taught by faculty and staff, who are trained.

There are also a few areas of great fluctuation (e.g., links to learning community, number of pre-professional seminars, teaching roles for administrators). Although these variations may reflect real changes, they could also be a result of the limited sample size and, in some cases, changes in the way a question was worded. Therefore, we suggest interpreting these data with caution.

Table 6.1

Comparison of Institutions Offering First-Year Seminars, 1988-2006

Institutions offering first-year seminars	1988 (*N* = 1,699)	1991 (*N* = 1,064)	1994 (*N* = 1,003)	1997 (*N* = 1,336)	2000 (*N* = 1,013)	2003 (*N* = 771)	2006 (*N* = 968)
Number	1,163	695	720	939	749	629	821
Percentage	68.5	65.4	71.8	70.3	73.9	81.6	84.8

Note. In 2003, the survey underwent significant revisions. In addition, the 2003 and 2006 surveys were administered via the Web.

Conclusion

As educators attempt to respond to increasingly diverse student populations with ever changing needs, the first-year seminar continues to play a critical role in helping students succeed. Though course elements or delivery methods may change over time, the goal of the seminar continues to be about helping all first-year students successfully adjust, learn, and progress to graduation. This monograph provides information that, we hope, will prove useful to anyone attempting to create or improve their first-year seminar and, most importantly, support first-year students.

Notes

[1] For more information on courses, refer to chapter 3.
[2] For more information on students, refer to chapter 3.
[3] For more information on instruction, refer to chapter 4.
[4] For more information on administration, refer to chapter 3.
[5] For more information on assessment, refer to chapter 5.

Table 6.2

Comparison of Survey Results, 1988-2006

	1988 (N = 1,163)	1991 (N = 695)	1994 (N = 720)	1997 (N = 939)	2000 (N = 748)	2003 (N = 629)	2006 (N = 821)
Seminar Types							
Extended orientation		71.0%	72.2%	68.7%	62.1%	65.2%	57.9%
Academic (uniform content)		12.1%	11.3%	10.5%	16.7%	27.4%	28.1%
Academic (variable content)		7.0%	7.8%	9.7%	12.8%	24.3%	25.7%
Basic study skills		6.0%	5.0%	5.7%	3.6%	20.0%	21.6%
Pre-professional		1.4%	1.3%	2.7%	2.7%	14.2%	14.9%
Hybrid							20.3%
Other		3.8%	3.8%	2.7%	2.1%	8.2%	4.4%
Seminar size							
Limit seminar size to 25 or less	45.9%[a]	68.1%	59.8%	68.4%	47.5%	86.9%	85.6%[b]
Require seminar for all first-year students	43.5%	45.0%	42.8%	46.9%	49.7%	46.8%	46.0%[b]
Grades and Credit							
Seminar assigned letter grade	61.9%	68.1%	75.4%	76.6%	81.7%	78.9%	82.0%[b]
Offer academic credit for seminar	82.2%	85.6%	86.1%	87.8%	90.0%	89.3%	92.2%[b]

Table 6.2 continued p. 101

Table 6.2 continued

	1988 (N = 1,163)	1991 (N = 695)	1994 (N = 720)	1997 (N = 939)	2000 (N = 748)	2003 (N = 629)	2006 (N = 821)
Apply Credit As							
Core requirement		19.4%	18.9%	19.8%	22.0%		
General education		28.7%	26.4%	27.1%	34.7%	57.3%	50.4%
Elective		45.4%	49.8%	45.6%	42.8%	42.0%	40.3%
Major requirement		2.4%	1.5%	3.1%	4.8%	6.0%	9.3%
Other		4.1%	3.4%	4.4%	6.0%	8.0%	6.1%
Seminar Instructor(s)							
Faculty		84.5%	85.0%	87.0%	88.9%	89.9%	90.0%
Student affairs professionals		50.8%	54.2%	60.4%	53.9%	45.3%	45.2%
Other campus administrators		34.1%	36.9%	41.0%	37.2%	30.9%	26.8%
Undergraduate students		8.1%	8.6%	9.0%	10.0%	6.3%	7.7%
Graduate students		4.2%	5.8%	6.0%	4.9%	4.4%	5.2%
Other		10.2%	9.2%	5.0%	3.3%	30.9%	26.8%
Advisors as instructors					20.1%	30.4%	31.9%
Assign Teaching of Seminar As							
Regular load for faculty		51.9%	53.2%	55.4%	57.8%	68.8%[b]	64.4%[b]
Overload for faculty		36.5%	38.2%	42.8%	40.1%	39.6%[b]	37.6%[b]
Regular load for administrators		25.2%	28.2%	25.7%	24.8%	41.7%[b]	30.7%[b]
Extra responsibility for administrators		31.7%	29.4%	36.2%	34.8%	58.9%[b]	42.5%[b]
Offer instructor training		71.4%	70.8%	75.9%	77.2%	72.4%	76.8%[b]
Require training for instructors		46.7%	48.2%	49.6%	49.4%	68.8%[b]	52.3%[b]
Seminar part of learning community			17.2%	14.1%	25.1%	24.8%	35.3%[b]
Program Longevity							
2 years or less	30.1%	23.8%	22.4%	16.7%	11.7%	8.7%	9.8%
10 years or less		81.4%	80.9%	72.3%	79.1%	58.9%	52.3%[b]
More than 10 years						41.1%	47.8%[b]

Note. Blank fields reflect questions not on survey or posed in a different manner in different administrations.

[a]Seminar limited to fewer than 20 students.

[b]The total population (*N*) reflects the number of institutions responding to the survey. However, once the survey was accessed via the Web, branching was used for many questions. Therefore, the number of institutions responding to this question was less than the reported *N*.

About the Authors

Barbara F. Tobolowsky is associate director of the National Resource Center for The First-Year Experience and Students in Transition. In this position, she has overall responsibility for the Center's research, publication, and conference efforts. Tobolowsky is also a clinical faculty member in the Higher Education and Student Affairs program at the University of South Carolina and has taught University 101, the first-year seminar at South Carolina. She earned her doctorate from the University of California, Los Angeles in higher education and organizational change.

Angela M. Griffin is the coordinator of research, grants, and assessment at the National Resource Center for The First-Year Experience and Students in Transition. She earned her bachelor's degree from the University of North Carolina at Chapel Hill and master's and doctoral degrees in developmental psychology from The University of Texas at Austin. Angela is responsible for the Center's research and grants efforts. She also serves as editor of the FYA-List essay series, a listserv series dedicated to assessment in the first college year.

Jonathan Romm worked as the graduate assistant for research at the National Resource Center for The First-Year Experience and Students in Transitions in 2007-08. He holds a B.S. in biochemistry from Marquette University and an M.Ed. from the University of South Carolina. Jonathan is currently working as the program coordinator for North Carolina Campus Compact, based at Elon University. His research interests include first-generation college students, civic engagement, and service-learning.

Dana Fish Saunders worked as a graduate assistant at the National Resource Center for The First-Year Experience and Students in Transition in 2007-08. She earned a B.A. in psychology and sociology from Roanoke College and an M.Ed. from the University of South Carolina. Dana is currently an assistant director for student academic services at the University of North Carolina at Greensboro. Her research interests include the transfer student transition, the first-year experience, and students dealing with academic difficulty.

Asheley Schryer is the coordinator of tutoring and academic recovery programs in the Student Success Center at the University of South Carolina. She has also worked at New Mexico State University in the Center for Learning Assistance. Asheley has a B.A. in English from New Mexico State University and her M.Ed. in Higher Education and Student Affairs from the University of South Carolina.

Appendix A

National Survey on First-Year Seminars 2006

This survey is dedicated to gathering information regarding first-year seminars. The survey should take approximately 20 minutes to complete. You may exit the survey at any time and return, and your responses will be saved. The survey will reopen on the first page. If you would like a copy of your responses, you will need to print each page of your survey before exiting. Your responses are important to us, so please respond by December 31, 2006. Thank you.

Background Information

Name of Institution: _____

Your Name: _____

Title: _____

Department Address: _____

City: _____

State: _____

Zip Code: _____

Telephone: _____

First-year seminars are courses designed to enhance the academic skills and/or social development of first-year college students.

Does your institution, including any department or division, offer one or more first-year seminar-type courses?

☐ Yes   ☐ No

Mark the appropriate categories regarding your institution:

☐ Two-year institution   ☐ Public
☐ Four-year institution   ☐ Private

Institution selectivity (entrance difficulty level):

☐ High
☐ Moderate
☐ Low

What is the approximate undergraduate enrollment (head count) at your institution? (Only numeric input, please.)_____

What is the approximate number of entering first-year students at your institution? (Only numeric input, please.) _____

What is the approximate percentage of first-year students who participate in a first-year seminar course? (Only numeric input, please.) _____

Types of Seminars Offered

Approximately how many years has a first-year seminar been offered on your campus?
- ☐ Two years or less
- ☐ Three to 10 years
- ☐ More than 10 years

Select each discrete type of first-year seminar that best describes the seminars that exist on your campus. (Select all that apply.)

- ☐ *Extended Orientation Seminar.* Sometimes called freshman orientation, college survival, college transition, or student success course. Content likely will include introduction to campus resources, time management, academic and career planning, learning strategies, and an introduction to student development issues.
- ☐ *Academic Seminar with generally uniform academic content across sections.* May be an interdisciplinary or theme-oriented course, sometimes part of a general education requirement. Primary focus is on academic theme/discipline, but will often include academic skills components such as critical thinking and expository writing.
- ☐ *Academic Seminar on various topics.* Similar to previously mentioned academic seminar except that specific topics vary from section to section.
- ☐ *Pre-Professional or Discipline-Linked Seminar.* Designed to prepare students for the demands of the major/discipline and the profession. Generally taught within professional schools or specific disciplines such as engineering, health sciences, business, or education.
- ☐ *Basic Study Skills Seminar.* Offered for academically underprepared students. The focus is on basic academic skills such as grammar, note taking, and reading texts, etc.
- ☐ *Hybrid.* Has elements from two or more types of seminar.
- ☐ *Other*

If you selected 'Hybrid,' please describe the type of first-year seminar. _____

_____

_____

If you selected 'Other,' please describe the type of first-year seminar. _____

_____

_____

_____

_____

Specific Seminar Information

If you offer more than one first-year seminar type, select the type with the highest total student enrollment to answer the remaining questions.

That seminar type is:

☐ Extended Orientation Seminar

☐ Academic Seminar with generally uniform content

☐ Academic Seminar on various topics

☐ Pre-Professional or Discipline-Linked Seminar

☐ Basic Study Skills Seminar

☐ Hybrid

☐ Other

Please indicate the approximate number of sections of this seminar type offered in the 2006-2007 academic year. (Only numerical input, please.)_____

Please answer the remaining questions for the seminar type with the highest student enrollment.

The Students

What is the approximate class size for each first-year seminar section?

☐ Under 10 students

☐ 10-15

☐ 16-20

☐ 21-25

☐ 26-30

☐ Over 30 (Specify approximate size below.)

Which students, by category, are required to take the first-year seminar? (Select all that apply.)

☐ None are required to take it.

☐ Honors students

☐ Learning community participants

☐ Provisionally admitted students

☐ Student athletes

☐ Students in specific majors

☐ Undeclared students

☐ Other _____

If you selected 'Students in specific majors,' please list the majors. _____

_____

_____

What is the approximate percentage of first-year students required to take the first-year seminar?

☐ None are required to take it.

☐ 100%

☐ 99%-90%

☐ 89%-80%

☐ 79%-70%

☐ 69%-60%

☐ 59%-50%

☐ Less than 50%

Are special sections of the first-year seminar offered for any of the following unique sub-populations of students? (Select all that apply.)

- ☐ No special sections are offered.
- ☐ Academically underprepared students
- ☐ Honors students
- ☐ International students
- ☐ Learning community participants
- ☐ Pre-professional students (i.e., pre-law, pre-med)
- ☐ Student athletes
- ☐ Students residing within a particular residence hall
- ☐ Students within a specific major
- ☐ Transfer students
- ☐ Undeclared students
- ☐ Other _____

If you selected 'Students within a specific major,' please list the majors. _____

_____

_____

The Instructors

Who teaches the first-year seminar? (Select all that apply.)

- ☐ Faculty
- ☐ Graduate students
- ☐ Undergraduate students
- ☐ Student affairs professionals
- ☐ Other campus professionals (Describe below.)

_____

If undergraduate students assist in the first-year seminar, how are they used? (Select all that apply.)

- ☐ They teach independently.   ☐ They assist the instructor, but do not teach.
- ☐ They teach as a part of a team.

Indicate the approximate percentage of sections that are team taught.

- ☐ No sections are team taught.   ☐ 74%-50%
- ☐ 100%   ☐ 49%-25%
- ☐ 99%-75%   ☐ Less than 25%

Please identify team configurations if they are used in your first-year seminar courses.

_____

_____

_____

Are any first-year students intentionally placed in first-year seminar sections taught by their academic advisors?

- ☐ Yes   ☐ No

If 'yes,' give the approximate percentage of students placed in sections with their academic advisors.

_____

For faculty, how is teaching the first-year seminar configured for workload? (Select all that apply.)
- ☐ As part of regular teaching load
- ☐ As an overload course
- ☐ Other _____

For student affairs or other campus professionals, how is teaching the first-year seminar configured for workload? (Select all that apply.)
- ☐ As an assigned responsibility
- ☐ As an extra responsibility
- ☐ Other _____

If taught as an overload or extra responsibility, what type of compensation is offered for teaching a first-year seminar? (Select all that apply.)
- ☐ Stipend
- ☐ Release time
- ☐ Graduate student support
- ☐ Other _____

If you selected 'Stipend,' please indicate the amount. _____

If you selected 'Release time,' please indicate the amount. _____

If you selected 'Graduate student support,' please indicate the number of students/hours per week.

_____

Is instructor training *offered* for first-year seminar instructors?
- ☐ Yes   ☐ No

If 'Yes,' how long is instructor training?
- ☐ Half a day or less
- ☐ 1 day
- ☐ 2 days
- ☐ 3 days
- ☐ 4 days
- ☐ 1 week
- ☐ Other _____

Is instructor training *required* for first-year seminar instructors?
- ☐ Yes   ☐ No

The Course
This first-year seminar is offered for:
- ☐ One semester
- ☐ One quarter
- ☐ One year
- ☐ Other _____

How is the first-year seminar graded?
- ☐ Pass/fail   ☐ No grade
- ☐ Letter grade

How many total classroom contact hours are there per week in the first-year seminar?
- ☐ One   ☐ Four
- ☐ Two   ☐ Five
- ☐ Three   ☐ More than five

Does the first-year seminar carry academic credit?
- ☐ Yes   ☐ No

If 'Yes,' how many credits does the first-year seminar carry?
- ☐ One   ☐ Four
- ☐ Two   ☐ Five
- ☐ Three   ☐ More than five

How may such credit apply? (Select all that apply).
- ☐ As an elective
- ☐ Toward general education requirements
- ☐ Toward major requirements
- ☐ Other _____

Do any sections include a service-learning component (i.e., non-remunerative service as part of a course)?
- ☐ Yes   ☐ No

If 'Yes,' please describe the component. _____

Are any sections linked to one or more other courses (i.e., "learning community"—enrolling a cohort of student into two or more courses)?
- ☐ Yes   ☐ No

If 'Yes,' please describe the section. _____

Do any sections incorporate online components?
- ☐ Yes   ☐ No

If 'Yes,' please describe the online components. _____

Are there any online-only sections?
- ☐ Yes   ☐ No

If 'Yes,' please indicate the approximate percentage of online-only sections. _____

Select the three most important *course objectives* for the first-year seminar.
- ☐ Create common first-year experience
- ☐ Develop academic skills
- ☐ Develop support network/friendships
- ☐ Improve sophomore return rates
- ☐ Increase student/faculty interaction
- ☐ Introduce a discipline
- ☐ Provide orientation to campus resources and services
- ☐ Self-exploration/personal development
- ☐ Encourage arts participation
- ☐ Other

If 'Other,' please describe the course objective for the first-year seminar. _____

Select the *three* most important topics that compose the content of this first-year seminar.
- ☐ Academic planning/advising
- ☐ Career exploration/preparation
- ☐ Campus resources
- ☐ College policies and procedures
- ☐ Critical thinking
- ☐ Diversity issues
- ☐ Relationship issues (e.g., interpersonal skills, conflict resolution)
- ☐ Specific disciplinary topic
- ☐ Study skills
- ☐ Time management
- ☐ Writing skills
- ☐ Other

If 'Other,' please describe the topics used to compose the content of the first-year seminar.

_____

Please list up to *three* elements or aspects of your first-year seminar that you consider innovative or especially successful.

_____

_____

The Administration

What campus unit directly administers the first-year seminar?
- ☐ Academic affairs
- ☐ Academic department
- ☐ First-year program office
- ☐ Student affairs
- ☐ Other _____

If you selected 'Academic Department,' please specify the academic department.

_____

Is there a dean/director/coordinator of the first-year seminar?

☐ Yes   ☐ No

If yes, is this position:

☐ Full-time (approximately 40 hours per week)   ☐ Less than full-time

If you selected 'Less than full time,' does the dean/director/coordinator have another position on campus?

☐ Yes   ☐ No

The dean/director/coordinator's other campus role is as a/an:

☐ Academic affairs administrator
☐ Faculty member
☐ Student affairs administrator
☐ Other _____

Evaluation Results

Has your first-year seminar been formally assessed or evaluated since fall 2003?

☐ Yes   ☐ No

What type of evaluation was conducted?

Focus groups with instructors	☐ Yes	☐ No	☐ I don't know
Focus groups with students	☐ Yes	☐ No	☐ I don't know
Individual interviews with instructors	☐ Yes	☐ No	☐ I don't know
Individual interviews with students	☐ Yes	☐ No	☐ I don't know
Student course evaluation	☐ Yes	☐ No	☐ I don't know
Survey instrument	☐ Yes	☐ No	☐ I don't know
Use of collected institutional data	☐ Yes	☐ No	☐ I don't know

If other than the types of evaluation listed above, please describe.

_____

Did your institution create a survey instrument?

☐ Yes   ☐ No

Did your institution use an established instrument?

☐ Yes   ☐ No

If you used an established instrument, please identify. (Select all that apply.)

☐ First-Year Initiative (FYI)
☐ National Survey of Student Engagement (NSSE)
☐ Your First College Year (YFCY)
☐ Other

If 'Other,' please describe the survey instrument used. _____

What were the outcomes of your assessment and research? (Select all that apply.)
- ☐ Improved grade-point average
- ☐ Improved peer connections with peers
- ☐ Increased academic abilities
- ☐ Increased level of student participation in campus activities
- ☐ Increased out-of-class student/faulty interaction
- ☐ Increased persistence to graduation
- ☐ Increased persistence to sophomore year
- ☐ Increased student satisfaction with faculty
- ☐ Increased student satisfaction with the institution
- ☐ Increased student use of campus services
- ☐ Other

If 'Other,' please describe the outcomes of your assessment and research.

_____

Survey Responses

It is our practice to make available to all requesting institutions specific and general information gathered from this survey.

Please select the appropriate response.

☐ You may share my survey responses.   ☐ Please do not share my survey responses.

Appendix B

Respondents to the 2006 National Survey on First-Year Seminars[1]

Abilene Christian University	Abilene	Texas
AIB College of Business	Des Moines	Iowa
Aims Community College	Greeley	Colorado
Alaska Pacific University	Anchorage	Alaska
Albany State University	Albany	Georgia
Albion College	Albion	Michigan
Alcorn State University	Alcorn State	Mississippi
Alfred University	Alfred	New York
Allegany College of Maryland	Cumberland	Maryland
Allegheny College	Meadville	Pennsylvania
American International College	Springfield	Massachusetts
Appalachian Bible College	Bradley	West Virginia
Aquinas College	Grand Rapids	Michigan
Arizona Western College	Yuma	Arizona
Arkansas Northeastern College	Blytheville	Arkansas
Arkansas State University	State University	Arkansas
Asheville-Buncombe Technical Community College	Asheville	North Carolina
Ashland University	Ashland	Ohio
Athens Technical College	Athens	Georgia
Augusta State University	Augusta	Georgia
Aurora University	Aurora	Illinois
Austin College	Sherman	Texas
Austin Peay State University	Clarksville	Tennessee
Avila University	Kansas City	Missouri
Babson College	Babson Park	Massachusetts
Baker College	Auburn Hills	Michigan
Baldwin-Wallace College	Berea	Ohio
Bard College	Annandale	New York
Barton College	Wilson	North Carolina
Beacon College	Leesburg	Florida
Belmont Abbey College	Belmont	North Carolina
Belmont University	Nashville	Tennessee

Beloit College	Beloit	Wisconsin
Benedict College	Columbia	South Carolina
Bennett College	Greensboro	North Carolina
Bentley College	Waltham	Massachusetts
Bergen Community College	Paramus	New Jersey
Berry College	Mount Berry	Georgia
Bethany College	Bethany	West Virginia
Bethany Lutheran College	Mankato	Minnesota
Bethel College	North Newton	Kansas
Bethel College (Indiana)	Mishawaka	Indiana
Bethune-Cookman College	Daytona Beach	Florida
Big Sandy Community and Technical College	Prestonsburg	Kentucky
Binghamton University	Binghamton	New York
Biola University	La Mirada	California
Birmingham-Southern College	Birmingham	Alabama
Blackburn College	Carlinville	Illinois
Blue Mountain College	Blue Mountain	Mississippi
Blue Mountain Community College	Pendleton	Oregon
Boise State University	Boise	Idaho
Boston Architectural College	Boston	Massachusetts
Bowdoin College	Brunswick	Maine
Brandeis University	Waltham	Massachusetts
Bridgewater College	Bridgewater	Virginia
Brigham Young University	Provo	Utah
Bristol Community College	Fall River	Massachusetts
Buena Vista University	Strom Lake	Iowa
Buffalo State College	Buffalo	New York
California Lutheran University	Thousand Oaks	California
California Polytechnic State University	San Luis Obispo	California
California State Polytechnic University, Pomona	Pomona	California
California State University, Chico	Chico	California
California State University, Dominguez Hill	Carson	California
California State University, East Bay	Hayward	California
California State University, Monterey Bay	Seaside	California
Canisius College	Buffalo	New York
Capital Community College	Hartford	Connecticut
Cardinal Stritch University	Milwaukee	Wisconsin
Carlow University	Pittsburgh	Pennsylvania
Carroll College	Helena	Montana
Carroll College	Waukesha	Wisconsin
Carroll Community College	Westminster	Maryland
Carson-Newman College	Jefferson City	Tennessee
Case Western Reserve University	Cleveland	Ohio
Cazenovia College	Cazenovia	New York
Cedarville University	Cedarville	Ohio
Central Bible College	Springfield	Missouri
Central College	Pella	Iowa
Central Michigan University	Mount Pleasant	Michigan

Centre College	Danville	Kentucky
Chapman University	Orange	California
Christian Brothers University	Memphis	Tennessee
Christopher Newport University	Newport News	Virginia
Cincinnati State Technical and Community College	Cincinnati	Ohio
Citrus College	Glendale	California
Claflin University	Orangeburg	South Carolina
Clarion University of Pennsylvania	Clarion	Pennsylvania
Clark College	Vancouver	Washington
Clark University	Worcester	Massachusetts
Clayton State University	Morrow	Georgia
Clearwater Christian College	Clearwater	Florida
Cleary University	Ann Arbor	Michigan
Clemson University	Clemson	South Carolina
Cloud County Community College	Concordia	Kansas
Coastal Carolina University	Conway	South Carolina
Coe College	Cedar Rapids	Iowa
Coffeyville Community College	Coffeyville	Kansas
College Misericordia	Dallas	Pennsylvania
College of Mount St. Joseph	Cincinnati	Ohio
College of Notre Dame of Maryland	Baltimore	Maryland
College of Saint Elizabeth	Morristown	New Jersey
College of Saint Mary	Omaha	Nebraska
College of St. Benedict's/St. John's University	Collegeville	Minnesota
College of The Albemarle	Elizabeth City	North Carolina
College of the Atlantic	Bar Harbor	Maine
College of the Southwest	Hobbs	New Mexico
Colorado College	Colorado Springs	Colorado
Colorado State University-Pueblo	Pueblo	Colorado
Columbia Basin College	Pasco	Washington
Columbia College	Columbia	South Carolina
Columbia College Chicago	Chicago	Illinois
Columbia University	New York	New York
Community Christian College	Redlands	California
Concordia University	Austin	Texas
Concordia University, St. Paul	St. Paul	Minnesota
Coppin State University	Baltimore	Maryland
Cornell College	Mount Vernon	Iowa
Craven Community College	New Bern	North Carolina
Cuyamaca College	El Cajon	California
Dakota State University	Madison	South Dakota
Dana College	Blair	Nebraska
Dartmouth College	Hanover	New Hampshire
Davis & Elkins College	Elkins	West Virginia
Dean College	Franklin	Massachusetts
Deep Springs College	Dyer	Nevada
Delaware County Community College	Media	Pennsylvania
Delaware State University	Dover	Delaware

Delta State University	Cleveland	Mississippi
Denison University	Granville	Ohio
DePaul University	Chicago	Illinois
Dixie State College	St. George	Utah
Doane College	Crete	Nebraska
Dordt College	Sioux Center	Iowa
Drexel University	Philadelphia	Pennsylvania
Drury University	Springfield	Missouri
Dyersburg State Community College	Dyersburg	Tennessee
East Central University	Ada	Oklahoma
East Georgia College	Swainsboro	Georgia
East Texas Baptist University	Marshall	Texas
Eastern Connecticut State University	Willimantic	Connecticut
Eastern Kentucky University	Richmond	Kentucky
Eastern Nazarene College	Quincy	Massachusetts
Eastern New Mexico University	Portales	New Mexico
Eastern New Mexico University-Roswell	Roswell	New Mexico
Edgecombe Community College	Tarboro	North Carolina
Edgewood College	Madison	Wisconsin
Edison Community College	Piqua	Ohio
Elgin Community College	Elgin	Illinois
Elizabethtown College	Elizabethtown	Pennsylvania
Elmhurst College	Elmhurst	Illinois
Elms College	Chicopee	Massachusetts
Elon University	Elon	North Carolina
Emerson College	Boston	Massachusetts
Emmanuel College	Boston	Massachusetts
Emory & Henry College	Emory	Virginia
Endicott College	Beverly	Massachusetts
Erie Community College	Williamsville	New York
Erskine College	Due West	South Carolina
Essex County College	Newark	New Jersey
Evangel University	Springfield	Missouri
Fairleigh Dickinson University	Teaneck	New Jersey
Fairmont State University	Fairmont	West Virginia
Fayetteville State University	Fayetteville	North Carolina
Ferrum College	Ferrum	Virginia
Finlandia University	Hancock	Michigan
Fisk University	Nashville	Tennessee
Florence-Darlington Technical College	Florence	South Carolina
Florida Atlantic University	Boca Raton	Florida
Florida Institute of Technology	Melbourne	Florida
Florida Southern College	Lakeland	Florida
Fontbonne University	St. Louis	Missouri
Fort Hays State University	Hays	Kansas
Fort Lewis College	Durango	Colorado
Framingham State College	Framingham	Massachusetts
Franklin College	Franklin	Indiana

Franklin Pierce College	Rindge	New Hampshire
Frederick Community College	Frederick	Maryland
Front Range Community College	Longmont	Colorado
Front Range Community College	Fort Collins	Colorado
Fullerton College	Fullerton	California
GateWay Community College	Phoenix	Arizona
Georgia College & State University	Milledgeville	Georgia
Georgia Southern University	Statesboro	Georgia
Georgia State University	Atlanta	Georgia
Georgian Court University	Lakewood	New Jersey
Gettysburg College	Gettysburg	Pennsylvania
Glendale Community College	Glendale	Arizona
Glenville State College	Glenville	West Virginia
Gordon College	Wenham	Massachusetts
Grace College	Winona Lake	Indiana
Graceland University	Lamoni	Iowa
Grambling State University	Grambling	Louisiana
Grand Valley State University	Allendale	Michigan
Greenville College	Greenville	Illinois
Gustavus Adolphus College	Saint Peter	Minnesota
Hanover College	Hanover	Indiana
Harcum College	Bryn Mawr	Pennsylvania
Harvey Mudd College	Claremont	California
Hawaii Pacific University	Honolulu	Hawaii
Henderson Community College	Henderson	Kentucky
Henderson State University	Arkadelphia	Arkansas
Hendrix College	Conway	Arkansas
Highland Community College	Freeport	Illinois
Hiram College	Hiram	Ohio
Hobart and William Smith Colleges	Geneva	New York
Hocking College	Nelsonville	Ohio
Holy Family University	Philadelphia	Pennsylvania
Holy Names University	Oakland	California
Hope College	Holland	Michigan
Hope International University	Fullerton	California
Hudson County Community College	Jersey City	New Jersey
Humboldt State University	Arcata	California
Huntington University	Huntington	Indiana
Illinois College	Jacksonville	Illinois
Illinois State University	Normal	Illinois
Immaculata University	Immaculata	Pennsylvania
Indiana Institute of Technology	Fort Wayne	Indiana
Indiana University East	Richmond	Indiana
Indiana University Kokomo	Kokomo	Indiana
Indiana University Southeast	New Albany	Indiana
Indiana Wesleyan University	Marion	Indiana
Institute of American Indian Arts	Santa Fe	New Mexico
Inver Hills Community College	Inver Grove Heights	Minnesota

Isothermal Community College	Spindale	North Carolina
Ithaca College	Ithaca	New York
Ivy Tech Community College of Indiana	Terre Haute	Indiana
Ivy Tech Community College of Indiana	Sellersburg	Indiana
Ivy Tech Community College of Indiana, Bloomington	Bloomington	Indiana
Ivy Tech Community College, Kokomo	Kokomo	Indiana
Jackson State Community College	Jackson	Tennessee
Jackson State University	Jackson	Mississippi
James Madison University	Harrisonburg	Virginia
Jamestown College	Jamestown	North Dakota
Jarvis Christian College	Hawkins	Texas
Jefferson College of Health Sciences	Roanoke	Virginia
John Carroll University	University Heights	Ohio
John Jay College of Criminal Justice, CUNY	New York	New York
Johnson County Community College	Overland Park	Kansas
Johnson State College	Johnson	Vermont
Judson College	Elgin	Illinois
Kalamazoo College	Kalamazoo	Michigan
Kansas State University	Manhattan	Kansas
Kapi`olani Community College	Honolulu	Hawaii
Kean University	Union	New Jersey
Kennesaw State University	Kennesaw	Georgia
Kent State University	Kent	Ohio
Kentucky State University	Frankfort	Kentucky
Keuka College	Keuka Park	New York
Kingsborough Community College	Brooklyn	New York
La Sierra University	Riverside	California
Lackawanna College	Scranton	Pennsylvania
Lake City Community College	Lake City	Florida
Lake Erie College	Painesville	Ohio
Lake Michigan College	Benton Harbor	Michigan
Lake Superior State University	Sault Ste. Marie	Michigan
Lake-Sumter Community College	Leesburg	Florida
Lamar Institute of Technology	Beaumont	Texas
Landmark College	Putney	Vermont
Lansing Community College	Lansing	Michigan
Lasell College	Newton	Massachusetts
Lawrence Technological University	Southfield	Michigan
Lawrence University	Appleton	Wisconsin
Le Moyne College	Syracuse	New York
Lebanon Valley College	Annville	Pennsylvania
Lee University	Cleveland	Tennessee
Lenoir Community College	Kinston	North Carolina
Lesley University	Cambridge	Massachusetts
Lewis & Clark College	Portland	Oregon
Lewis University	Romeoville	Illinois
Life Pacific College	San Dimas	California
Lon Morris College	Jacksonville	Texas

Longwood University	Farmville	Virginia
Loras College	Dubuque	Iowa
Lord Fairfax Community College	Middletown	Virginia
Los Angeles Pierce College	Woodland Hills	California
Louisburg College	Louisburg	North Carolina
Louisiana State University, Alexandria	Alexandria	Louisiana
Lower Columbia College	Longview	Washington
Loyola University New Orleans	New Orleans	Louisiana
Lyme Academy College of Fine Arts	Old Lyme	Connecticut
Lyndon State College	Lyndonville	Vermont
Lynn University	Boca Raton	Florida
Macalester College	St. Paul	Minnesota
MacMurray College	Jacksonville	Illinois
Madonna University	Livonia	Michigan
Malone College	Canton	Ohio
Manchester College	North Manchester	Indiana
Manhattanville College	Purchase	New York
Mansfield University	Mansfield	Pennsylvania
Marian College	Indianapolis	Indiana
Marion Technical College	Marion	Ohio
Marshall Community and Technical College	Huntington	West Virginia
Martin Methodist College	Pulaski	Tennessee
Marymount University	Arlington	Virginia
Maryville College	Maryville	Tennessee
Massachusetts Institute of Technology	Cambridge	Massachusetts
McHenry County College	Crystal Lake	Illinois
McNeese State University	Lake Charles	Louisiana
Medaille College	Kenmore	New York
Mercer University	Macon	Georgia
Mercyhurst College	Erie	Pennsylvania
Metropolitan State College of Denver	Denver	Colorado
Miami University (Ohio)	Oxford	Ohio
Mid-America Christian University	Oklahoma City	Oklahoma
Middle Georgia College	Cochran	Georgia
Middle Tennessee State University	Murfreesboro	Tennessee
Middlesex Community College	Bedford	Massachusetts
Middlesex County College	Edison	New Jersey
Midwestern State University	Wichita Falls	Texas
Millersville University	Millersville	Pennsylvania
Millsaps College	Jackson	Mississippi
Milwaukee Area Technical College	Milwaukee	Wisconsin
Minneapolis Community and Technical College	Minneapolis	Minnesota
Minnesota State College-Southeast	Winona	Minnesota
Missouri Southern State University	Joplin	Missouri
Missouri State University	Springfield	Missouri
Mohawk Valley Community College	Utica	New York
Monmouth College	Monmouth	Illinois
Monmouth University	West Long Branch	New Jersey

Montclair State University	Montclair	New Jersey
Monterey Peninsula College	Monterey	California
Montgomery College	Germantown	Maryland
Montreat College	Montreat	North Carolina
Moraine Park Technical College	Fond du Lac	Wisconsin
Morningside College	Sioux City	Iowa
Morris College	Sumter	South Carolina
Mount Mary College	Milwaukee	Wisconsin
Mount St. Mary's College	Los Angeles	California
Mount St. Mary's University	Emmitsburg	Maryland
Mount Union College	Alliance	Ohio
Mount Vernon Nazarene University	Mount Vernon	Ohio
Mt. Hood Community College	Gresham	Oregon
Muhlenberg College	Allentown	Pennsylvania
Muskingum College	New Concord	Ohio
Naropa University	Boulder	Colorado
Nassau Community College	Garden City	New York
Naugatuck Valley Community College	Waterbury	Connecticut
New Jersey Institute of Technology	Newark	New Jersey
New Mexico Highlands University	Las Vegas	New Mexico
New Mexico Junior College	Hobbs	New Mexico
New Mexico Military Institute	Roswell	New Mexico
New Mexico State University	Las Cruces	New Mexico
New Mexico State University, Carlsbad	Carlsbad	New Mexico
New York Institute of Technology	New York	New York
Niagara University	Niagara University	New York
Nichols College	Dudley	Massachusetts
North Carolina Central University	Durham	North Carolina
North Central State College	Mansfield	Ohio
North Greenville University	Tigerville	South Carolina
North Hennepin Community College	Brooklyn Park	Minnesota
Northern Illinois University	DeKalb	Illinois
Northern Michigan University	Marquette	Michigan
Northland College	Ashland	Wisconsin
NorthWest Arkansas Community College	Bentonville	Arkansas
Northwest Christian College	Eugene	Oregon
Northwest Nazarene University	Nampa	Idaho
Northwestern Connecticut Community College	Winsted	Connecticut
Northwestern Technical College	Rock Spring	Georgia
Northwood University	Midland	Michigan
Norwalk Community College	Norwalk	Connecticut
Oakland University	Rochester	Michigan
Oberlin College	Oberlin	Ohio
Ocean County College	Toms River	New Jersey
Oglethorpe University	Atlanta	Georgia
Ohio Dominican University	Columbus	Ohio
Ohio State University at Lima	Lima	Ohio
Ohio University Southern	Ironton	Ohio

Oklahoma Panhandle State University	Goodwell	Oklahoma
Oklahoma State University	Stillwater	Oklahoma
Oregon State University	Corvallis	Oregon
Ottawa University	Ottawa	Kansas
Pacific University	Forest Grove	Oregon
Palo Alto College	San Antonio	Texas
Panola College	Carthage	Texas
Parkland College	Champaign	Illinois
Patten University	Oakland	California
Paul Smith's College	Paul Smiths	New York
Peace College	Raleigh	North Carolina
Penn State University at Mont Alto	Mont Alto	Pennsylvania
Pepperdine University	Malibu	California
Peru State College	Peru	Nebraska
Philadelphia Biblical University	Langhorne	Pennsylvania
Pine Manor College	Chestnut Hill	Massachusetts
Plymouth State University	Plymouth	New Hampshire
Portland State University	Portland	Oregon
Potomac State College of West Virginia University	Keyser	West Virginia
Princeton University	Princeton	New Jersey
Purchase College	Purchase	New York
Quincy University	Quincy	Illinois
Quinebaug Valley Community College	Danielson	Connecticut
Ramapo College	Mahwah	New Jersey
Raritan Valley Community College	North Branch	New Jersey
Reading Area Community College	Reading	Pennsylvania
Reed College	Portland	Oregon
Regis College	Denver	Colorado
Regis College	Weston	Massachusetts
Rhode Island College	Providence	Rhode Island
Richard Stockton College	Pomona	New Jersey
Rider University	Lawrenceville	New Jersey
Riverland Community College	Austin	Minnesota
Robert Morris University	Moon Township	Pennsylvania
Roberts Wesleyan College	Rochester	New York
Rochester Institute of Technology	Rochester	New York
Rollins College	Winter Park	Florida
Roosevelt University	Schaumburg	Illinois
Rose State College	Midwest City	Oklahoma
Rose-Hulman Institute of Technology	Terre Haute	Indiana
Rosemont College	Rosemont	Pennsylvania
Rowan University	Glassboro	New Jersey
Saint Francis University	Loretto	Pennsylvania
Saint Joseph College	West Hartford	Connecticut
Saint Joseph's University	Philadelphia	Pennsylvania
Saint Leo University	Saint Leo	Florida
Saint Louis University	St. Louis	Missouri
Saint Martin's University	Lacey	Washington

Saint Mary-of-the-Woods College	Saint Mary-of-the-Woods	Indiana
Saint Mary's University of Minnesota	Winona	Minnesota
Saint Michael's College	Colchester	Vermont
Saint Paul's College	Lawrenceville	Virginia
Salem College	Winston-Salem	North Carolina
Salve Regina University	Newport	Rhode Island
Sam Houston State University	Huntsville	Texas
Samford University	Birmingham	Alabama
San Jose State University	San Jose	California
Santa Barbara City College	Santa Barbara	California
Seton Hall University	South Orange	New Jersey
Seward County Community College	Liberal	Kansas
Shepherd University	Shepherdstown	West Virginia
Shorter College	Rome	Georgia
Silver Lake College	Manitowoc	Wisconsin
Simmons College	Boston	Massachusetts
Sitting Bull College	Fort Yates	North Dakota
Skidmore College	Saratoga Springs	New York
Snead State Community College	Boaz	Alabama
Snow College	Ephraim	Utah
South Dakota School of Mines and Technology	Rapid City	South Dakota
South Dakota State University	Brookings	South Dakota
South Florida Community College	Avon Park	Florida
South Puget Sound Community College	Olympia	Washington
Southeast Missouri State University	Cape Girardeau	Missouri
Southeastern Community College	Whiteville	North Carolina
Southern Illinois University	Carbondale	Illinois
Southern Illinois University Edwardsville	Edwardsville	Illinois
Southern Nazarene University	Bethany	Oklahoma
Southern Oregon University	Ashland	Oregon
Southern State Community College	Hillsboro	Ohio
Southern Utah University	Cedar City	Utah
Southwest Georgia Technical College	Thomasville	Georgia
Southwest Minnesota State University	Marshall	Minnesota
Southwestern Adventist University	Keene	Texas
Southwestern University	Georgetown	Texas
Spartanburg Methodist College	Spartanburg	South Carolina
Spelman College	Atlanta	Georgia
Spring Arbor University	Spring Arbor	Michigan
Spring Hill College	Mobile	Alabama
Springfield College	Springfield	Massachusetts
Springfield College in Illinois	Springfield	Illinois
St. Ambrose University	Davenport	Iowa
St. Gregory's University	Shawnee	Oklahoma
St. John's University	Queens	New York
St. Joseph's College	Brooklyn	New York
St. Lawrence University	Canton	New York
St. Thomas University	Miami Gardens	Florida

State University of New York at Fredonia	Fredonia	New York
State University of New York College at Cobleskill	Cobleskill	New York
State University of New York College at Geneseo	Geneseo	New York
State University of New York College at Oneonta	Oneonta	New York
State University of New York College at Oswego	Oswego	New York
State University of New York College at Plattsburgh	Plattsburgh	New York
State University of New York College of Environmental Sciences and Forestry	Syracuse	New York
State University of New York College of Technology at Delhi	Delhi	New York
Stephen F. Austin State University	Nacogdoches	Texas
Stillman College	Tuscaloosa	Alabama
Stonehill College	N. Easton	Massachusetts
Stony Brook University	Stony Brook	New York
Suffolk University	Boston	Massachusetts
Sullivan County Community College	Loch Sheldrake	New York
Tacoma Community College	Tacoma	Washington
Tallahassee Community College	Tallahassee	Florida
Tarleton State University	Stephenville	Texas
Tarrant County College - NE Campus	Hurst	Texas
Taylor University	Upland	Indiana
Tennessee State University	Nashville	Tennessee
Texas A&M International University	Laredo	Texas
Texas A&M University-Corpus Christi	Corpus Christi	Texas
Texas A&M University-Kingsville	Kingsville	Texas
Texas Christian University	Fort Worth	Texas
Texas Southern University	Houston	Texas
Texas State Technical College Harlingen	Harlingen	Texas
Texas State Technical College West Texas	Sweetwater	Texas
Texas State University-San Marcos	San Marcos	Texas
Texas Wesleyan University	Fort Worth	Texas
The Citadel	Charleston	South Carolina
The College of Mount Saint Vincent	Bronx	New York
The College of New Jersey	Ewing	New Jersey
The Master's College	Newhall	California
The Ohio State University	Columbus	Ohio
The University of Akron	Akron	Ohio
The University of Central Oklahoma	Edmond	Oklahoma
The University of Texas at Brownsville	Brownsville	Texas
The University of West Alabama	Livingston	Alabama
Thomas College	Waterville	Maryland
Thomas More College	Crestview Hills	Kentucky
Thomas University	Thomasville	Georgia
Tougaloo College	Tougaloo	Mississippi
Tri-State University	Angola	Indiana
Trinity College	Hartford	Connecticut
Troy University	Troy	Alabama
Truman State University	Kirksville	Missouri

Tulane University	New Orleans	Louisiana
Tusculum College	Greeneville	Tennessee
Union College	Barbourville	Kentucky
Union College	Schenectady	New York
Unity College	Unity	Maine
University at Buffalo	Buffalo	New York
University of Alabama at Birmingham	Birmingham	Alabama
University of Alaska Anchorage	Anchorage	Alaska
University of Alaska Southeast	Juneau	Alaska
University of Arkansas Community College	Hope	Arkansas
University of Arkansas Community College	Morrilton	Arkansas
University of Arkansas, Little Rock	Little Rock	Arkansas
University of California, Berkeley	Berkeley	California
University of California, Davis	Davis	California
University of California, Los Angeles	Los Angeles	California
University of California, San Diego	La Jolla	California
University of California, Santa Cruz	Santa Cruz	California
University of Central Florida	Orlando	Florida
University of Colorado at Denver and Health Sciences Center	Denver	Colorado
University of Colorado, Colorado Springs	Colorado Springs	Colorado
University of Evansville	Evansville	Indiana
University of Great Falls	Great Falls	Montana
University of Kansas	Lawrence	Kansas
University of Kentucky	Lexington	Kentucky
University of La Verne	La Verne	California
University of Louisiana	Lafayette	Louisiana
University of Maine at Farmington	Farmington	Maine
University of Maine at Fort Kent	Fort Kent	Maine
University of Michigan	Ann Arbor	Michigan
University of Michigan-Dearborn	Dearborn	Michigan
University of Minnesota	Minneapolis	Minnesota
University of Missouri at Kansas City	Kansas City	Missouri
University of Missouri at St. Louis	St. Louis	Missouri
University of Nebraska-Kearney	Kearney	Nebraska
University of New Haven	West Haven	Connecticut
University of New Mexico	Albuquerque	New Mexico
University of New Mexico-Taos	Taos	New Mexico
University of North Carolina, Greensboro	Greensboro	North Carolina
University of North Carolina, Pembroke	Pembroke	North Carolina
University of North Dakota	Grand Forks	North Dakota
University of Oklahoma	Norman	Oklahoma
University of Pittsburgh at Bradford	Bradford	Pennsylvania
University of Pittsburgh at Greensburg	Greensburg	Pennsylvania
University of Pittsburgh at Johnstown	Johnstown	Pennsylvania
University of Portland	Portland	Oregon
University of Rio Grande	Rio Grande	Ohio
University of Rochester	Rochester	New York

University of Scranton	Scranton	Pennsylvania
University of South Alabama	Mobile	Alabama
University of South Carolina, Aiken	Aiken	South Carolina
University of South Carolina, Sumter	Sumter	South Carolina
University of South Dakota	Vermillion	South Dakota
University of Southern Indiana	Evansville	Indiana
University of Southern Maine	Portland	Maine
University of Tennessee, Martin	Martin	Tennessee
University of Texas at Arlington	Arlington	Texas
University of Texas at Austin	Austin	Texas
University of Texas at Tyler	Tyler	Texas
University of Texas of the Permian Basin	Odessa	Texas
University of Texas-Pan American	Edinburg	Texas
University of the Cumberlands	Williamsburg	Kentucky
University of the Ozarks	Clarksville	Arkansas
University of the Pacific	Stockton	California
University of the Sciences in Philadelphia	Philadelphia	Pennsylvania
University of Utah	Salt Lake City	Utah
University of Washington	Seattle	Washington
University of West Florida	Pensacola	Florida
University of Wisconsin - Eau Claire	Eau Claire	Wisconsin
University of Wisconsin - La Crosse	La Crosse	Wisconsin
University of Wisconsin - Milwaukee	Milwaukee	Wisconsin
University of Wisconsin - Stevens Point	Stevens Point	Wisconsin
University of Wisconsin Colleges	Waukesha	Wisconsin
University of Wyoming	Laramie	Wyoming
Upper Iowa University	Fayette	Iowa
Utah State University	Logan	Utah
Utica College	Utica	New York
Valdosta State University	Valdosta	Georgia
Valencia Community College	Orlando	Florida
Valley Forge Christian College	Phoenixville	Pennsylvania
Victoria College	Victoria	Texas
Villanova University	Villanova	Pennsylvania
Virginia Intermont College	Bristol	Virginia
Virginia Union University	Richmond	Virginia
Virginia Wesleyan College	Norfolk	Virginia
Viterbo University	La Crosse	Wisconsin
Wagner College	Staten Island	New York
Wallace Community College - Dothan	Enterprise	Alabama
Wallace State Community College	Hanceville	Alabama
Walsh University	North Canton	Ohio
Wartburg College	Waverly	Iowa
Washburn University	Topeka	Kansas
Washington & Jefferson College	Washington	Pennsylvania
Washington College	Chestertown	Maryland
Washington State Community College	Marietta	Ohio
Washington State University	Pullman	Washington

Waycross College	Waycross	Georgia
Wayland Baptist University	Plainview	Texas
Waynesburg College	Waynesburg	Pennsylvania
Webster University	St. Louis	Missouri
West Kentucky Community and Technical College	Paducah	Kentucky
West Liberty State College	West Liberty	West Virginia
West Virginia University Institute of Technology	Montgomery	West Virginia
Western Carolina University	Cullowhee	North Carolina
Western Kentucky University	Bowling Green	Kentucky
Western New England College	Springfield	Massachusetts
Western New Mexico University	Silver City	New Mexico
Western Technical College	La Crosse	Wisconsin
Westfield State College	Westfield	Massachusetts
Westminster College Missouri	Fulton	Missouri
Whatcom Community College	Bellingham	Washington
Wheaton College	Norton	Massachusetts
Wheeling Jesuit University	Wheeling	West Virginia
Whitman College	Walla Walla	Washington
Whitworth College	Spokane	Washington
Wichita State University	Wichita	Kansas
Wiley College	Marshall	Texas
William Beneke	Fayette	Missouri
William Jewell College	Liberty	Missouri
William Penn University	Oskaloosa	Iowa
William Woods University	Fulton	Missouri
Williamsburg Technical College	Kingstree	South Carolina
Wilson College	Chambersburg	Pennsylvania
Winston-Salem State University	Winston-Salem	North Carolina
Winthrop University	Rock Hill	South Carolina
Wofford College	Spartanburg	South Carolina
Worcester State College	Worcester	Massachusetts
Wright State University	Dayton	Ohio
Yale University	New Haven	Connecticut
York Technical College	Rock Hill	South Carolina
Youngstown State University	Youngstown	Ohio
Zane State College	Zanesville	Ohio

Notes

[1] This is a partial list of respondents, as 180 institutions asked not to be identified.